DRAW
INSECTS

by Doug DuBosque

PEEL productions, inc.

Supplies...

Find a **comfortable place to draw** – with decent light, so you can see what you're doing.

As you start to learn about insect anatomy, shapes and proportions, don't worry too much about materials.

Use a **pencil that's longer than your finger.** Also, think about using colored pencils.

Sharpen your pencil when it gets dull!

Get a **separate eraser.** My favorite is a *kneaded* type, available in art supply and craft stores (the eraser on your pencil will disappear quickly).

For practice drawings, use **recycled paper** – for example, draw on the back of old photocopies or computer printouts.

Always **draw lightly at first**, so you can erase problems as you need to.

Save your drawings and learn from them.

Enjoy drawing cool insects!

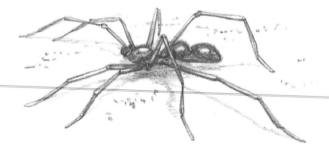

Copyright ©1998 Douglas C. DuBosque.

All rights reserved, including the right of reproduction in whole or in part, in any form.

Published by Peel Productions, Inc.

Printed in Singapove

Library of Congress Cataloging-in-Publication Data

DuBosque, D. C.
    Draw insects / by Doug DuBosque
        p.   cm.
        Summary: provides step-by-step instructions for drawing insects, including the bumblebee, giant beetle, and yellow jacket.
        ISBN 0-939217-28-7
        1. Insects in art--Juvenile literature. 2. Drawing--technique--Juvenile literature. [1. Insects in art. 2. Drawing--Technique.] I. Title.

NC783.D8   1997
743.6'57--dc21   97-44401

Distributed to the trade and art markets in North America by

NORTH LIGHT BOOKS,
an imprint of F&W Publications, Inc.
4700 East Galbraith Road
Cincinnati, OH 45236

(800) 289-0963

Contents

And now, a <u>brief</u> and <u>learned</u> discourse on insects:

The world of insects includes amazing diversity—and insects are *everywhere,* from frozen snow fields to inside other animals' bodies. Some feed on plants, some suck blood from mammals, and plenty of them eat other insects, spiders, and other creepy-crawlies.

So what is an insect?

Insects are those critters belonging to the class *Insecta,* in the phylum *Arthropoda* (arthropods). They live in all habitats. Arthropods have hard exoskeletons and jointed limbs–lobsters and crabs are arthropods, but they're not insects.

Insects have
- *six legs*
- *two antennae*
- *three body parts*
- *wings? Four, or two, or none at all.*

So think **6 legs.** And look for the other stuff as well.

OK, class dismissed!

You may now draw…

*P.S. The **darkened images** on each page show you the actual size of what you're drawing.*

Ant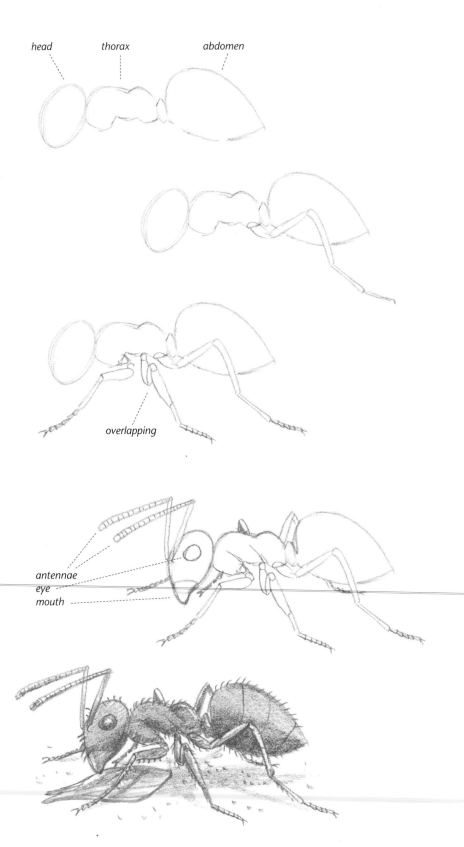

Order Hymenoptera
Family Formicidae

If you want to study insects, none are easier to find than ants! Their societies generally consist of wingless workers and winged reproducers. They live in underground nests or in dead wood. Most can 'bite' people if disturbed. Most ants scavenge, but some harvest seeds, cut leaves and farm fungus underground, or herd aphids to feed on their honeydew.

STUDY the final drawing *before you start!*

Do you see
- *three body parts?*
- *six legs?*
- *two antennae?*
- *wings?*
- *eyes?*

1. Draw the oval shape of the *head,* the peanut shape of the *thorax,* and the pointy oval shape of the *abdomen.*

2. Add the rear leg. *How many sections do you see?*

3. Draw the middle leg, and the front leg. Notice how the sections of the middle leg *overlap* to create depth.

4. Add *antennae, eye,* and *mouth.* Add the small visible bits of the other legs.

5. Add shading and texture. Draw a little tidbit and a cast shadow beneath the ant. Clean up any smudges with your eraser.

Great ant! To make your drawing more realistic, draw about a zillion of them, crawling all over the place....

head   thorax   abdomen

overlapping

antennae
eye
mouth

Aphid

Order Homoptera
Family Aphididae

Ask any gardener about aphids! These little plant-suckers appear in large numbers on leaves and stems of plants, leaving them wilted and curled. They can also spread plant diseases. Aphids give birth to young during spring and summer, and lay eggs to last through the winter. Ants help the process by gathering the eggs, storing them during the winter, then transporting the aphids from one food plant to another during the spring. Why? Because aphids also secrete something called honeydew, which the ants eat.

STUDY the final drawing *before you start!*

Do you see
  • *distinct body parts?*
  • *six legs?*
  • *two antennae?*
  • *wings?*
  • *eyes?*

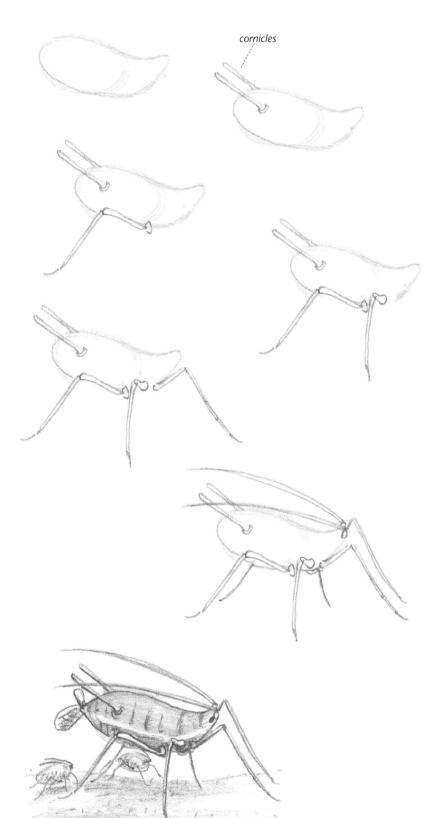

cornicles

1. Draw the body, almost pear-shaped.

2. Add the distinctive *cornicles* at the rear end of the aphid.

3. Draw the rear leg,…

4. …the middle leg,…

5. …and the front leg.

6. Add the antennae and eye.

7. Finish your drawing by shading and going over fine lines with a sharp pencil. Add a little plant stem and shadows.

Now add a little flap in the back and more baby aphids popping out, eager to devour your house plants….

Draw Insects   5

Assassin Bug

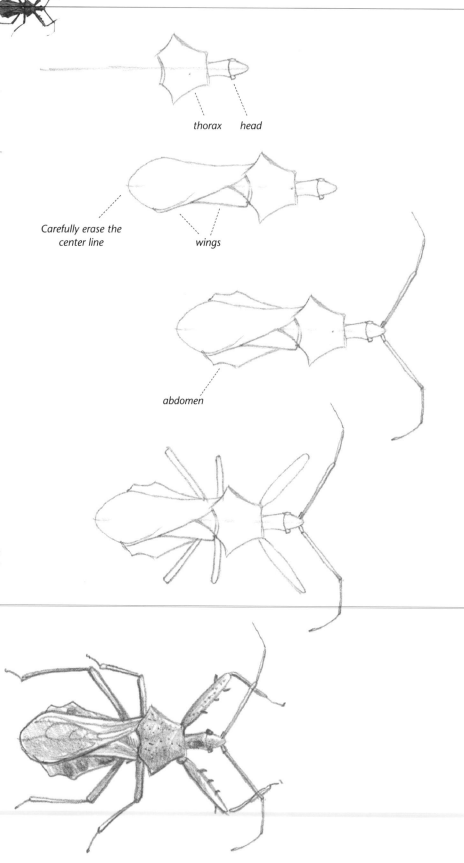

Order Hemiptera (true bugs)
Family Reduviidae

Assassin bugs have very strong front legs, which they use to grab and hold prey. They attack their victim with their short, sharp beaks and suck the body fluids out of them.

STUDY the final drawing *before you start!*

Do you see
- *three body parts?*
- *six legs?*
- *two antennae?*
- *wings?*
- *eyes?*

Does the insect look
- *shiny? smooth? fuzzy?*
- *hard? soft?*

1. Lightly draw the center line, and the six-sided *thorax.* Add the *head.*

2. Draw the *wings.*

3. Add the antennae, and the pointy shape of the *abdomen.*

4. Draw the first section of each leg. Which legs are the thickest and most powerful?

5. Carefully complete the legs. Draw veins in the wings. Add shading, texture, and details.

Idea! Draw another insect being attacked by the assassin bug....

thorax   head

Carefully erase the center line

wings

abdomen

eye

proboscis

Back Swimmer

Order Hemiptera (true bugs)
Family Notonectidae

Back swimmers use their legs to paddle on the surface of water. They also dive, and can stay under water up to six hours. They catch tadpoles, small aquatic insects, and insects that get caught in the water. Swimming on their backs, they have protective coloring similar to many fish: dark on the top side and light on the bottom.

STUDY the final drawing *before you start!*

Do you see
- *three body parts?*
- *six legs?*
- *two antennae?*
- *wings?*
- *eyes?*

Does the insect look
- *shiny? smooth? fuzzy?*
- *hard? soft?*

1. Lightly draw the centre line, then *eyes* and *proboscis,* and the rounded sides of the body.

2. Draw the first section of each leg.

3. Add remaining, feather-like sections to the back legs.

4. Draw remaining sections to front legs, and give your back swimmer a little snack to munch on.

5. Add shading, and a few little ripples to suggest water.

Floating in your pool, munching on a snack... what a life!

Bon appetit!

Bed Bug

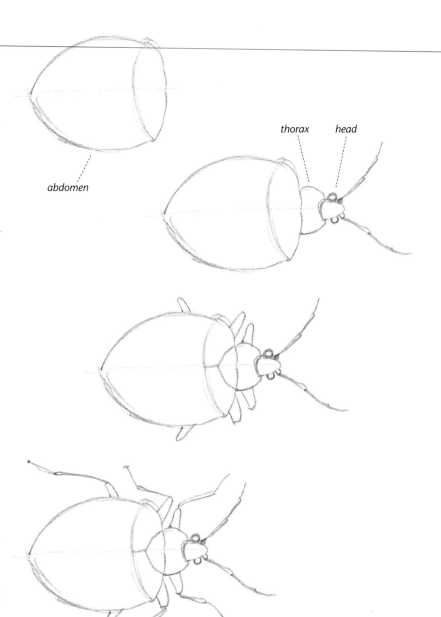

Order Hemiptera (true bugs)
Family Cimicidae

These flat, reddish-brown pests can really ruin a good night's sleep! They run surprisingly fast, and hunt for sleeping animals and birds at night when they can't find you. If they don't find anything, well, that's OK: adults have been known to live for a year without food.

STUDY the final drawing *before you start!*

Do you see
- *three body parts?*
- *six legs?*
- *two antennae?*
- *wings?*
- *eyes?*

Does the insect look
- *shiny? smooth? fuzzy?*
- *hard? soft?*

1. Draw the acorn-shaped *abdomen.*

2. Add the *thorax* and *head,* with beady little eyes looking for the best place to attack you in your sleep. Add antennae.

3. Draw the first segment of all six legs.

4. Add the remaining segments to each leg.

5. Add shading, texture, and stubbly little hairs, and a *cast shadow.*

Sleep tight!

Don't let the bedbugs bite!

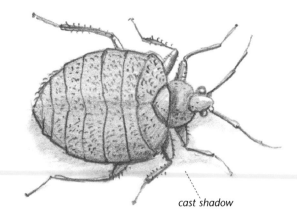

cast shadow

Black Fly

Order Diptera
Family Simuliidae

Black flies lay their eggs in streams and rivers. The larvae pupate in cocoons attached to rocks in the water. The adults burst out, rise on a bubble of air, and go forth to drive people crazy with their bites, in late spring or early summer. Some species transmit a type of malaria that kills ducks, geese, swans and turkeys.

STUDY the final drawing *before you start!*

Do you see
- *three body parts?*
- *six legs?*
- *two antennae?*
- *wings (how many)?*
- *eyes?*

Does the insect look
- *shiny? smooth? fuzzy?*
- *hard? soft?*

1. Start by drawing the slightly tilted wing. Look carefully at the example and draw the outline, almost straight on one side and more curved on the other. Add veins.

2. Draw the curved top of the *thorax, head,* eye and smaller details on the head.

3. Add two legs.

4. Draw the rear leg. Now add the segmented abdomen. Next, draw the legs on the far side of the fly.

5. Add shading and a bit of *cast shadow.* Shade the body and eye, leaving light areas to show the round forms. Lightly draw the outline of the other wing, and add shading and a *cast shadow.*

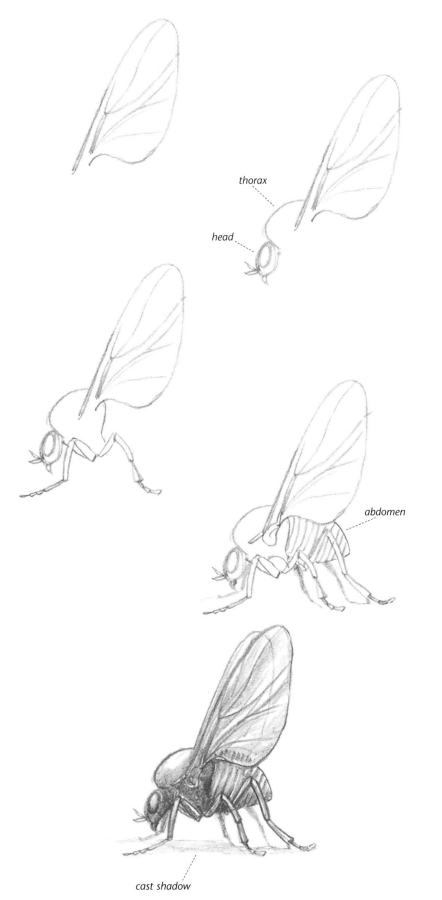

thorax

head

abdomen

cast shadow

Bumble Bee

Order Hymenoptera
Family Apidae

Bumblebees usually live in cooler areas, where their thick hair protects them from the cold. Usually they build nests underground. Their very long proboscises can reach into the deepest flowers, and some depend almost completely on bumblebees for fertilization. When the English brought clover to New Zealand, for example, it didn't grow well until they imported bumblebees. The English biologist Charles Darwin made the suggestion.

STUDY the final drawing *before you start!*

Do you see
- *three body parts?*
- *six legs?*
- *two antennae?*
- *wings (how many)?*
- *eyes?*

Does the insect look
- *shiny? smooth? fuzzy?*
- *hard? soft?*

1. Draw the circle of the *thorax,* leaving white spaces on either side where the wings attach. Add the flattened oval of the *abdomen,* with lines showing segments.

2. Add head, eyes, and antennae.

3. Carefully outline one *fore wing* and *hind wing.*

4. Repeat on the other side, and add veins to the wings.

5. Now draw the six legs.

6. Add shading, shadow, and texture. Notice which parts of the body are darker, and which are lighter.

thorax

abdomen

fore wing

hind wing

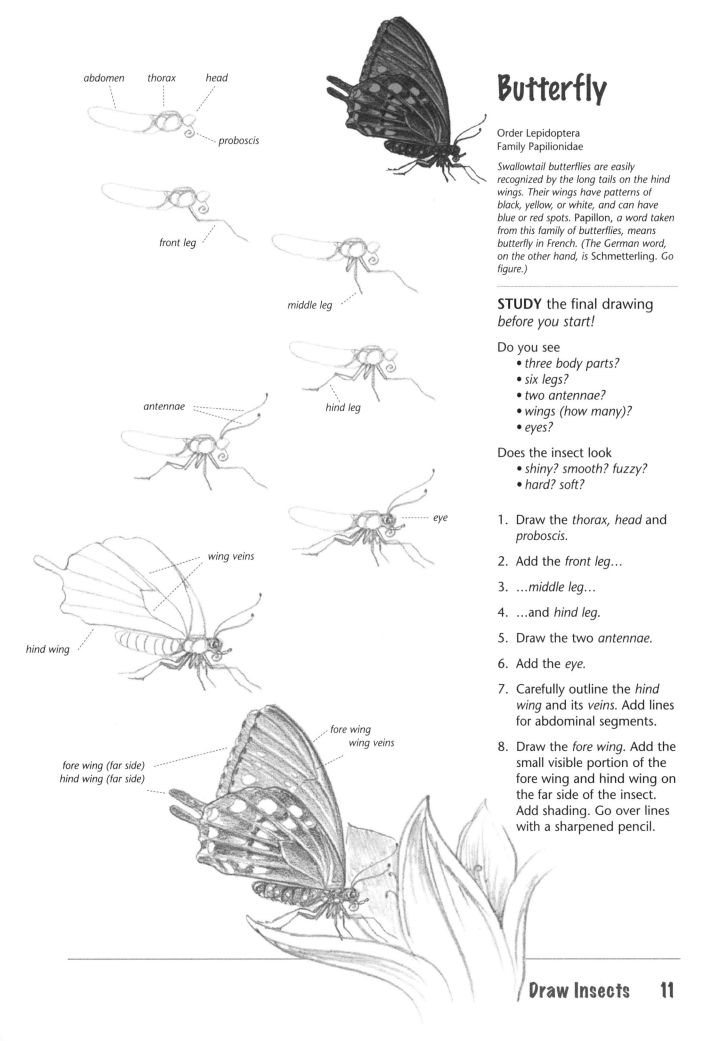

abdomen   thorax   head

proboscis

front leg

middle leg

antennae

hind leg

eye

wing veins

hind wing

fore wing (far side)
hind wing (far side)

fore wing
wing veins

Butterfly

Order Lepidoptera
Family Papilionidae

Swallowtail butterflies are easily recognized by the long tails on the hind wings. Their wings have patterns of black, yellow, or white, and can have blue or red spots. Papillon, a word taken from this family of butterflies, means butterfly in French. (The German word, on the other hand, is Schmetterling. Go figure.)

STUDY the final drawing *before you start!*

Do you see
- *three body parts?*
- *six legs?*
- *two antennae?*
- *wings (how many)?*
- *eyes?*

Does the insect look
- *shiny? smooth? fuzzy?*
- *hard? soft?*

1. Draw the *thorax, head* and *proboscis.*

2. Add the *front leg…*

3. …*middle leg…*

4. …and *hind leg.*

5. Draw the two *antennae.*

6. Add the *eye.*

7. Carefully outline the *hind wing* and its *veins.* Add lines for abdominal segments.

8. Draw the *fore wing.* Add the small visible portion of the fore wing and hind wing on the far side of the insect. Add shading. Go over lines with a sharpened pencil.

Caterpillar

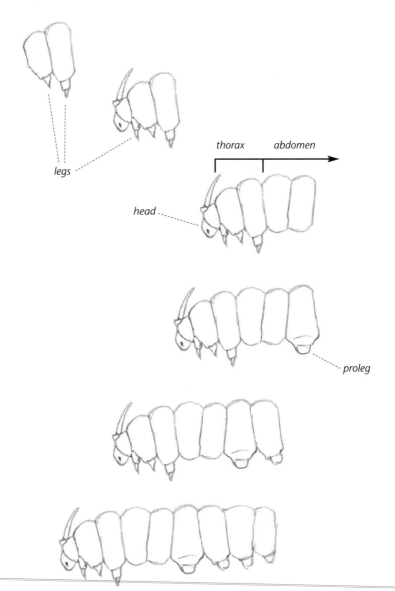

Order Lepidoptera

Caterpillars are young butterflies or moths. They may have horns, spines, and bristles; they show distinct colors and patterns. All caterpillars have three pairs of legs in the thorax, and up to five pairs of abdominal "prolegs."

STUDY the final drawing *before you start!*

Do you see
- *three body parts?*
- *six legs?*
- *two antennae?*
- *wings?*
- *eyes?*

Does the insect look
- *shiny? smooth? fuzzy?*
- *hard? soft?*

1. Draw two tall, rounded rectangles with tiny projections for *legs.*

2. Add a triangle shape and another leg, and small bump with a dot for the head. Draw a little horn on top.

3. Draw two more rounded rectangles of the *abdomen.*

4. Add another, with a little bump for a *proleg...*

5. ...and another...

6. ...and two more...

7. ...then three plain segments and a last segment with another proleg.

6. Now add pattern and shading, leaving a light area on each segment to make the caterpillar look shiny. And give it a little something to munch on!

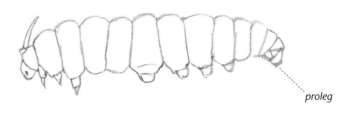

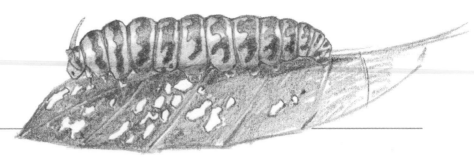

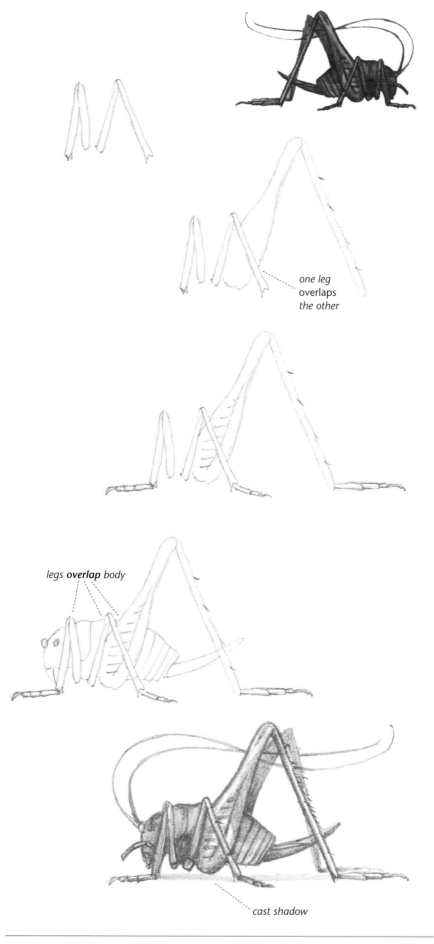

one leg
overlaps
the other

legs **overlap** body

cast shadow

Cave Cricket

Order Orthoptera
Family Gryllacrididae

Most crickets in this family have no wings. They live in caves and basements, or in dark places under logs, rocks, or bark. Some types make a scratchy sound, but most—unlike field crickets—make no sound at all. Their long antennae and leg bristles warn them of approaching predators, such as spiders or centipedes.

STUDY the final drawing *before you start!*

Do you see
- *three body parts?*
- *six legs?*
- *two antennae?*
- *wings?*
- *eyes?*

Does the insect look
- *shiny? smooth? fuzzy?*
- *hard? soft?*

1. Start with two bending legs forming an M shape.

2. Draw the powerful rear jumping leg behind.

3. Add additional segments to each leg, and the pattern on the largest leg.

4. Now draw the body behind the legs. Look carefully, and draw one part at a time.

   Because you drew the legs first, it's easy to show them overlapping *the body, adding depth to your drawing.*

5. Add shading, very long antennae, the other rear leg (shaded solid gray), and a slight *cast shadow*.

   Pretty cool looking critter!

Cicada

Order Homoptera
Family Cicadidae

Cicadas live in trees and make loud, pulsating buzzing sounds. They lay eggs on twigs, which usually die and fall to the ground. The nymph cicadas then feast on roots before crawling up a tree. Certain cicadas repeat this cycle only once every 13 or 17 years.

STUDY the final drawing *before you start!*

Do you see
- *three body parts?*
- *six legs?*
- *two antennae?*
- *wings (how many)?*
- *eyes?*

Does the insect look
- *shiny? smooth? fuzzy?*
- *hard? soft?*

1. Draw a rounded triangle with a little circle on the bottom and one side.

2. Add the peanut shape of the body on the other side of the triangle.

3. Outline the *fore wings.* Notice how one points down on the page, while the other points up at an angle.

4. Add the *hind wings.*

5. Carefully outline the veins in one wing. Take your time! Look carefully!

6. Complete your drawing by carefully adding veins to the other wings. Draw legs and segments of the body. Then add shading, and go over any fuzzy lines with a sharp pencil to make them look cleaner.

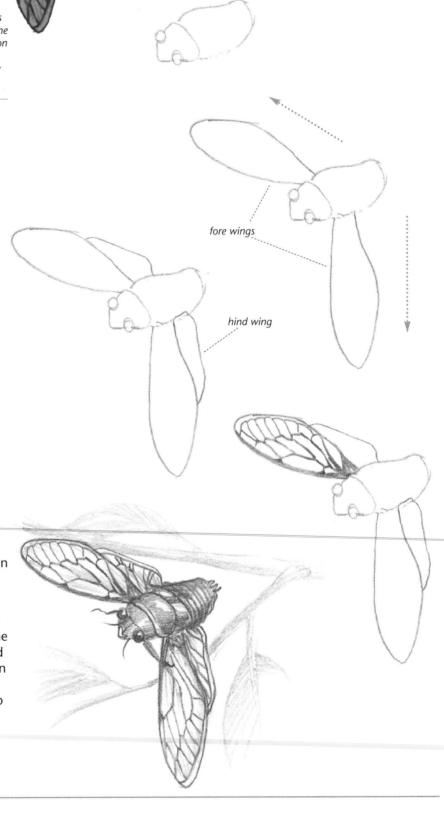

fore wings

hind wing

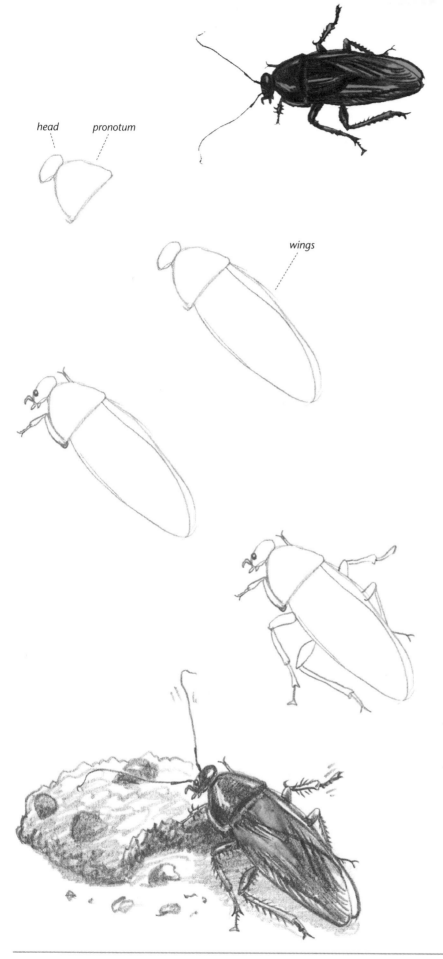

Cockroach

Order Blattodea
Family Blattidae

Cockroaches do not transmit human disease, but…they infest buildings, contaminate food, and have an unpleasant smell. They are active and fast runners at night; during the day they hide in cracks. They almost never fly, though they are among the oldest winged insects (350 million years). Some have become almost immune to pesticides after numerous attempts to eradicate them. And don't bother trying to starve them to death: some have lived for months on little more than dust!

STUDY the final drawing *before you start!*

Do you see
- *three body parts?*
- *six legs?*
- *two antennae?*
- *wings (how many)?*
- *eyes?*

Does the insect look
- *shiny? smooth? fuzzy?*
- *hard? soft?*

1. Draw a small flat oval for the *head* and a half-circle for the *pronotum.*

2. Add the long shape of the *wings.*

3. Draw details on the head, and add the visible bits of front legs.

4. Carefully add the remaining two pairs of legs.

5. Add antennae, bristly hairs on the legs, and shading.

For added realism, make your cockroach nibbling on a chocolate chip cookie!

Cow Killer

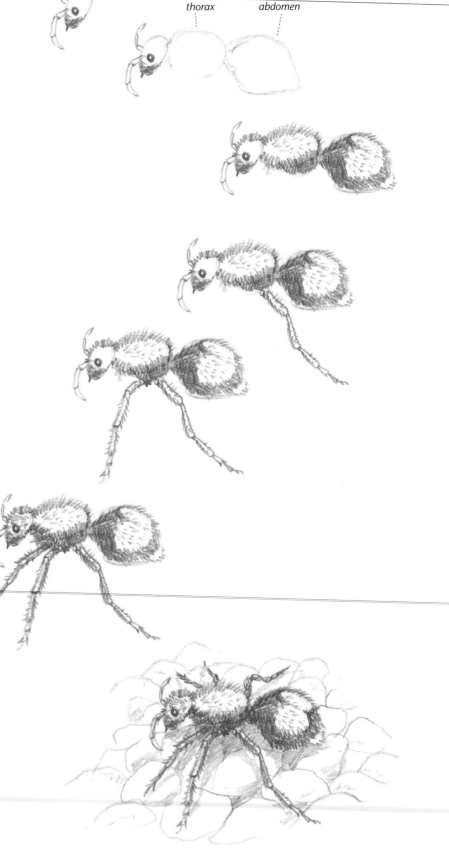

thorax abdomen

Order Hymenoptera
Family Mutillidae (Velvet-ants)

I had no idea this insect existed until I spotted one in the back yard while working on this book. It moved so fast I couldn't tell how many legs it had, and buzzed as it raced around. I'm glad I didn't try to pick it up: the sting from this wingless wasp is so painful that some people say it could kill a cow! Cow killers invade bumblebee nests and lay their eggs in them. They are bright red and black.

STUDY the final drawing *before you start!*

Do you see
- *three body parts?*
- *six legs?*
- *two antennae?*
- *wings?*
- *eyes?*

Does the insect look
- *shiny? smooth? fuzzy?*
- *hard? soft?*

1. Start with the oval shaped head, eye, and segmented antennae.

2. Draw two more oval shapes for the *thorax* and *abdomen*.

3. Add fuzzy hair covering the whole body. If you have colored pencils, make the light areas bright red, and the dark areas black.

4. Draw a long, bristly leg…

5. …and another…

6. …and another.

7. Finish your drawing by adding the other three legs, and some grains of sand or small pebbles, and a cast shadow beneath the body.

abdomen   thorax   eyes/head

Crane Fly

Order Diptera
Family Tipulidae

These flies seem to dance in midair. Larva feed on rotting vegetation and fungus, but adults don't eat at all! They live in humid areas, often near lakes or streams, and lay slender eggs in moist dirt.

STUDY the final drawing *before you start!*

Do you see
- *three body parts?*
- *six legs?*
- *two antennae?*
- *wings (how many)?*
- *eyes?*

Does the insect look
- *shiny? smooth? fuzzy?*
- *hard? soft?*

1. Draw the long, slender *abdomen* with lines dividing it into segments. Add the bulbous *thorax*, small pointy *head* and *eyes.*

2. Draw the two long wings, wing veins, and the tiny antennae.

3. Add the two very long rear legs.

4. Draw the middle legs, looking carefully at how they bend.

5. Add the front legs. Go over lines to darken them. Clean up any smudges with your eraser.

Deer Fly

Order Diptera
Family Tabanidae

This pest looks like a jet airplane when it lands after circling above its prey – and it feels like one too when it bites! As with horse flies and mosquitoes, only female deer flies feed on blood; the males drink plant juices. The larva feed on small aquatic insects. Some deer flies transmit bacteria that can cause tularemia in rabbits and hares…and occasionally people.

STUDY the final drawing *before you start!*

Do you see
  • *three body parts?*
  • *six legs?*
  • *two antennae?*
  • *wings (how many)?*
  • *eyes?*

Does the insect look
  • *shiny? smooth? fuzzy?*
  • *hard? soft?*

1. Starting with the *head* and two eyes, then add rounded rectangles of the *thorax* and *abdomen.*

2. Draw the wings, extending beyond the abdomen.

3. Add six legs, and antennae.

4. Look closely! Draw the markings on the back and the veins on the wings. Add markings on thorax and abdomen, and shade the eyes, leaving highlights.

5. Add shading to head, thorax, and abdomen. Shade the wings to make them look translucent: you can see shapes through them, but they're not completely clear.

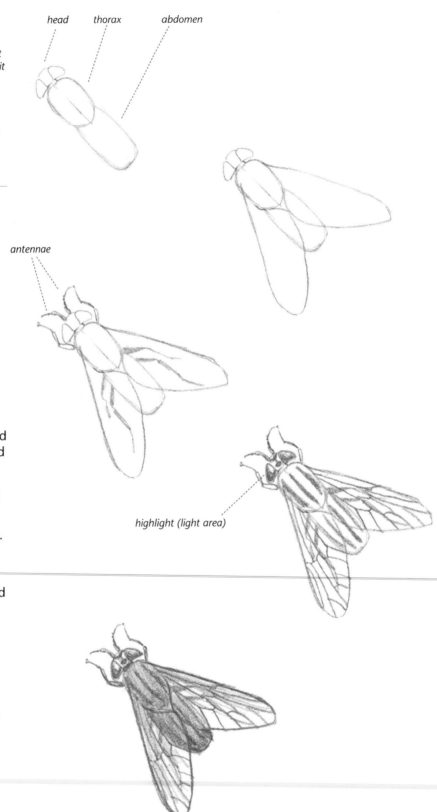

head   thorax   abdomen

antennae

highlight (light area)

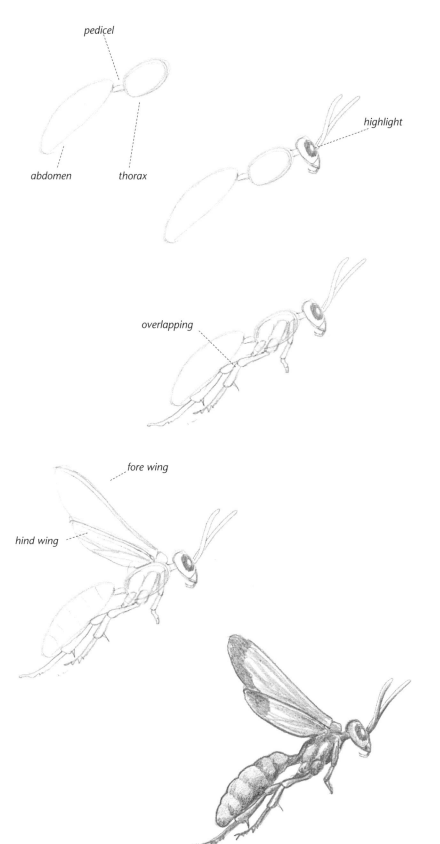

pedicel

abdomen   thorax

highlight

overlapping

fore wing

hind wing

Digger Wasp

Order Hymenoptera
Family Scoliidae (Scoliid Wasps)

Green June beetles have a good reason not to like digger wasps: the female wasps dig (possibly several feet) into the ground to find a beetle larva. Then she stings it, digs a little chamber around it and lays on egg on its back. When the egg hatches, the wasp larva eats the beetle larva.

STUDY the final drawing *before you start!*

Do you see
- *three body parts?*
- *six legs?*
- *two antennae?*
- *wings (how many)?*
- *eyes?*

1. Draw the long, tilted *abdomen* and rounder *thorax,* connected by the narrow *pedicel* (waist).

2. Add the head and neck, large eye with a highlight to make it look shiny. Draw mouth parts. Add antennae.

3. Carefully draw the legs, counting the sections of each. Notice how the middle leg *overlaps* the rear leg in flight.

4. Draw the wings (in this view, we see only the closer two). Make light guide lines to show the segments of the abdomen.

5. Add shading and texture.

Test question!
Why does a digger wasp dig?

Dragonfly

Order Odonata
Suborder Anisoptera

Dragonfly nymphs live in ponds and streams, so you often see adult dragonflies around water, though they can range several miles. Often brightly colored, dragonflies fly well and often, catching mosquitoes and midges in flight. They're fast! No wonder they have such big eyes!

STUDY the final drawing *before you start!*

Do you see
- *three body parts?*
- *six legs?*
- *two antennae?*
- *wings (how many)?*
- *eyes?*

Does the insect look
- *shiny? smooth? fuzzy?*
- *hard? soft?*

1. Start with two small circles for the *head* and *thorax,* and draw the long rectangle of the *abdomen.*

2. Draw one *hind wing*.

3. Add the *fore wing*.

4. Draw wings on the other side as well.

5. Add details on head, front legs, veins in wings, and lines on the abdomen.

6. Complete your drawing by adding more shading and about a zillion cells on each wing. Look closely at the example, and take your time drawing them!

   Dazzling dragonfly!

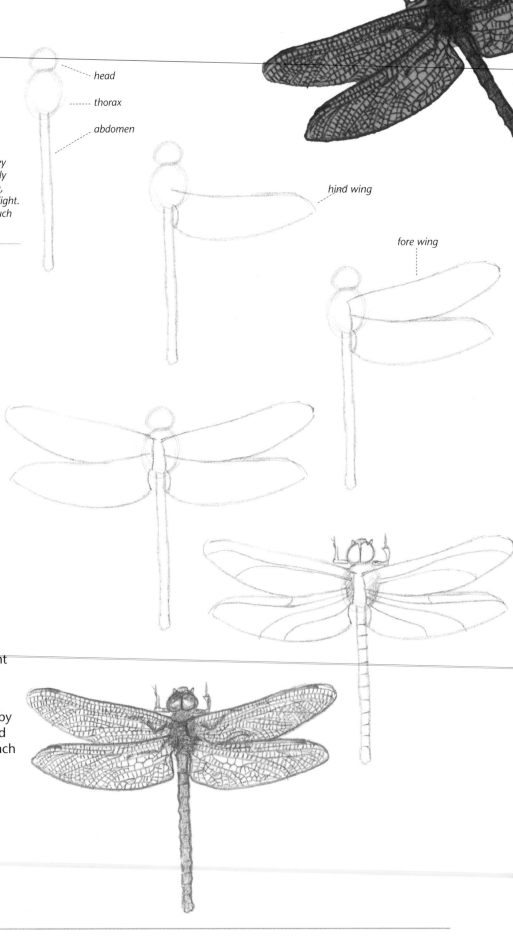

head

thorax

abdomen

hind wing

fore wing

Earwig

Order Dermaptera
Family Forficulidae

Their strange name comes from an old superstition that these insects got into people's ears (they don't...I don't think). They live and lay their eggs in plant debris, scavenging or feeding on plants at night. They use their pincerlike cerci in defense, and can pinch painfully. They also squirt a foul-smelling liquid if handled.

STUDY the final drawing *before you start!*

Do you see
- *three body parts?*
- *six legs?*
- *two antennae?*
- *wings (how many)?*
- *eyes?*

Does the insect look
- *shiny? smooth? fuzzy?*
- *hard? soft?*

1. Start by drawing the *head* and *thorax.*

2. Add the long *abdomen* with curving lines...

3. ...and add the nasty-looking *cerci* at the end.

4. Draw the rear legs...

5. ...the middle legs...

6. ...and then the front legs and segmented antennae.

7. Add shading, leaving light areas on the back to make the form look round.

I can understand the "ear" part, but where do you suppose the "wig" comes from?

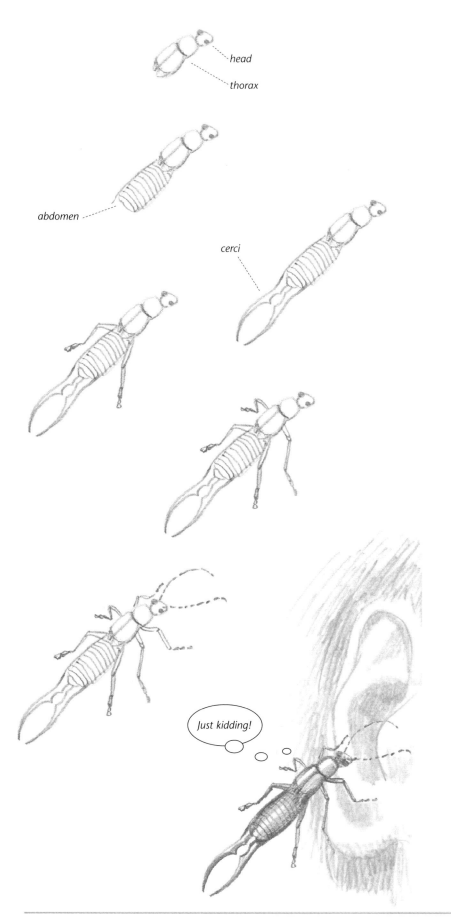

head

thorax

abdomen

cerci

Just kidding!

Firefly (Lightning Bug)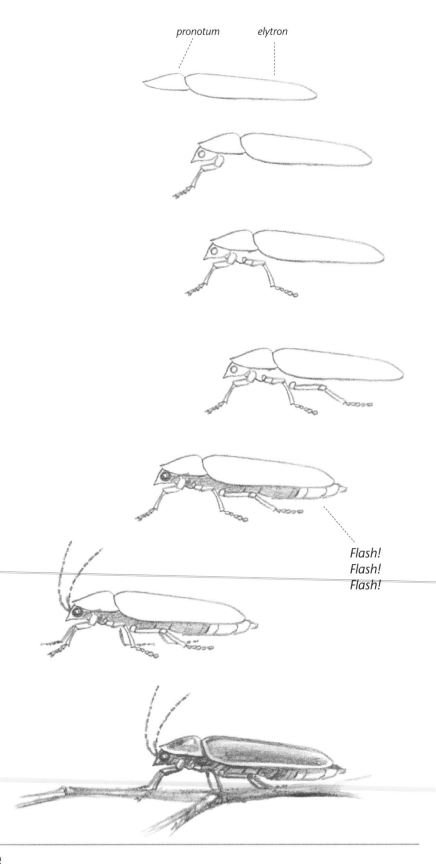

Order Coleoptera
Family Lampyridae

During spring and early summer, these beetles use their luminous abdominal sections to attract other fireflies for mating. Although other insects can glow, fireflies are unique in being able to flash, and the rhythms are distinct for each species. Active at night, they live under bark or in moist places under debris.

STUDY the final drawing *before you start!*

Do you see
- *three body parts?*
- *six legs?*
- *two antennae?*
- *wings (how many)?*
- *eyes?*

Does the insect look
- *shiny? smooth? fuzzy?*
- *hard? soft?*

1. Start by drawing the *pronotum* and *elytron* (one of two hard fore wings).

2. Draw the triangular head (almost completely covered by the *pronotum)* and the front leg.

3. Add the middle leg…

4. …and the rear leg.

5. Draw the body, and shade most of it dark. Leave the end of the abdomen light: this is the part that flashes. Make the eye dark, leaving a little reflective white spot.

6. Draw antennae, and the other three legs.

7. Carefully shade your drawing, leaving a light area at the top of the shiny protective shell. Draw a little branch for it to sit on.

pronotum elytron

Flash!
Flash!
Flash!

Flea

Order Siphonaptera
Family Pulicidae

Fleas are annoying parasites that live off the blood of their host; they lay eggs on their host or in its nest. Fleas help pets get tapeworm and can spread disease such as bubonic plague.

STUDY the final drawing *before you start!*

Do you see
- *three body parts?*
- *six legs?*
- *two antennae?*
- *wings?*
- *eye?*

1. Draw the head and first *thorax segment.*

2. Draw the front leg, attached to the first thorax segment. Count the sections of the leg, and look carefully at which direction each goes.

3. Draw the second thorax segment and middle leg, *behind* the front leg.

4. Draw the third thorax segment and powerful rear leg, *behind* the middle leg.

5. Add the top part of the abdomen…

6. …and the bottom.

7. Add *eye, antenna, palps,* three more legs, and shading. Don't forget the breathing *spiracles!*

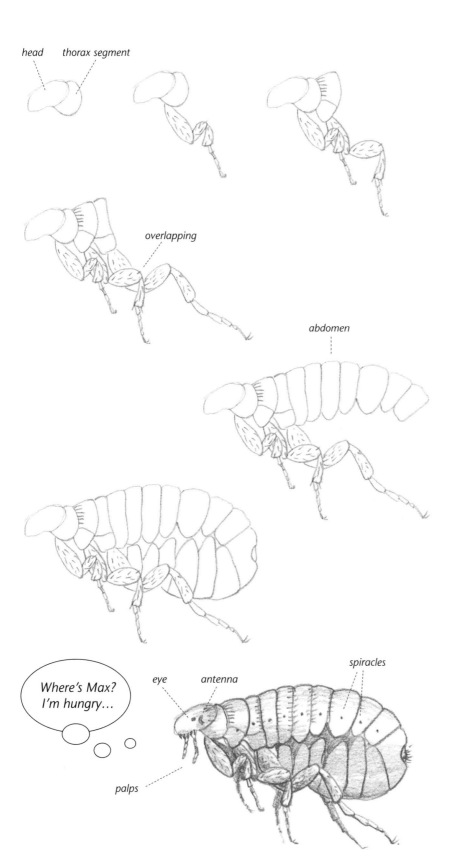

head   thorax segment

overlapping

abdomen

Where's Max? I'm hungry…

eye   antenna   spiracles

palps

Giant Beetle

Order Coleoptera
Family Scarabaeidae

Why do you suppose this is called the Giant Beetle? Put you hand over it to get an idea how big it is. Despite its scary-looking horns, this beetle wouldn't hurt you…in fact, it might feel kind of cool walking across your hand and up your arm….

STUDY the final drawing
before you start!

Do you see
- *three body parts?*
- *six legs?*
- *two antennae?*
- *wings (how many)?*
- *eyes?*

Does the insect look
- *shiny? smooth? fuzzy?*
- *hard? soft?*

1. Draw the front beetle wings *(elytra)* and *thorax.*

2. Add the *head* and ferocious-looking *horns.*

3. Draw the front legs.

4. Add the middle and hind legs.

5. Add the club-like antennae on either side of the center horn. Shade the beetle, leaving very light areas to make it look shiny. Go over lines with a sharp pencil. Use a dull pencil to add shading and a *cast shadow.*

   Awesome!

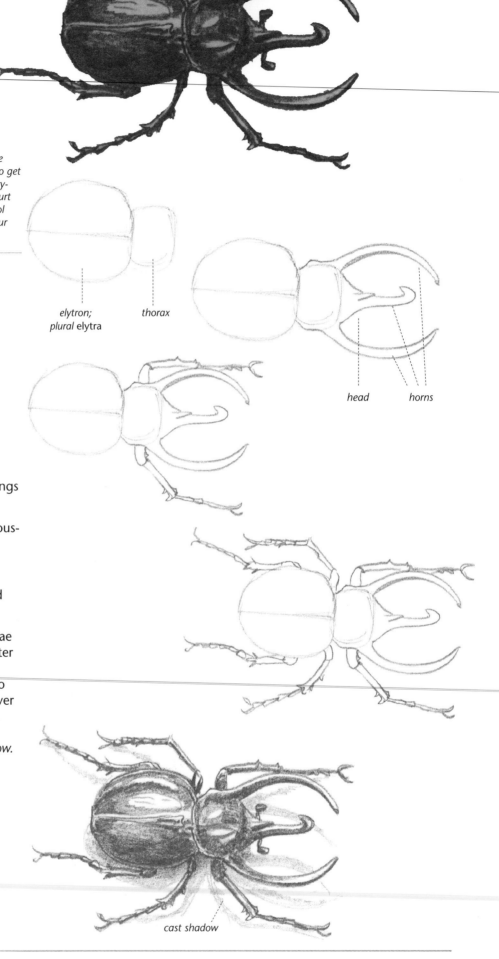

elytron;
plural elytra

thorax

head   horns

cast shadow

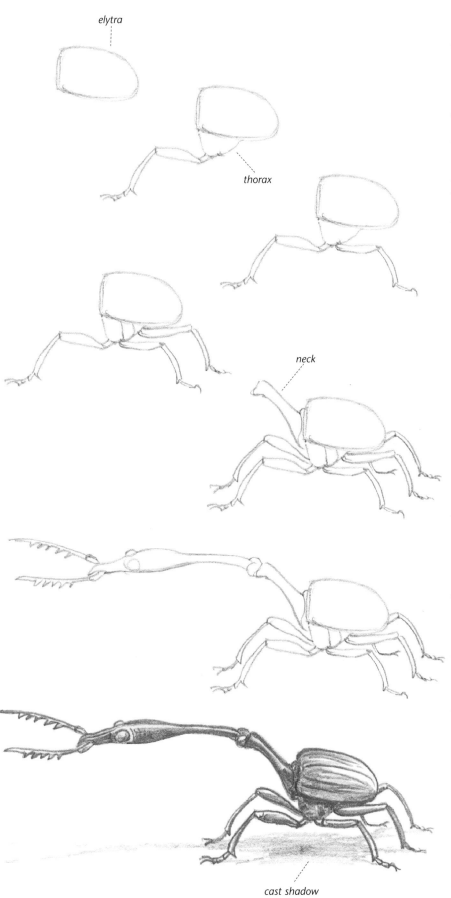

elytra

thorax

neck

Giraffe Beetle

Order Coleoptera
Family Curculionidae (snout beetles and weevils)
This little monster belongs to a group of hard-shelled beetles that chew holes in fruits, nuts, and other parts of plants. One member, the boll weevil, is well known for destroying cotton crops in the southern U.S. after accidental introduction from Mexico.

STUDY the final drawing
before you start!

Do you see
  • *three body parts?*
  • *six legs?*
  • *two antennae?*
  • *wings?*
  • *eyes?*

Does the insect look
  • *shiny? smooth? fuzzy?*
  • *hard? soft?*

1. Draw the flattened oval shape of the *elytra* (protective fore wings).

2. Draw the visible triangle of the *thorax.* Look carefully, then add the front leg,…

3. …the rear leg,…

4. …and the middle leg. Add lines to show the segments of the thorax.

5. Add visible parts of other legs, and the first section of the *neck.*

6. Now draw the rest of the neck and head.

7. Add shading, texture, and a *cast shadow* to complete your drawing.

   "Why is the neck on this beetle so long?" you ask. Good question!

cast shadow

Horse Fly

Order Diptera
Family Tabanidae

As with mosquitoes and deer flies, only female horse flies feed on blood, while the males eat pollen and nectar from flowers. Quieter than house flies, horse flies sneak up and give a nasty bite that continues to bleed because of an anticoagulant in the fly's saliva. A horse or cow can actually suffer serious blood loss if a number of horse flies attack it.

STUDY the final drawing *before you start!*

Do you see
  • *three body parts?*
  • *six legs?*
  • *two antennae?*
  • *wings (how many)?*
  • *eyes?*

Does the insect look
  • *shiny? smooth? fuzzy?*
  • *hard? soft?*

1. Start with a light *guide line* for the center of the fly. Add *abdomen, thorax,* and those *big green eyes.*

2. Draw the wings.

3. Add the six legs and two antennae.

4. Draw lines for abdominal segments and veins in wings. Add shading and texture. Add enough shading on the wings to make them appear *translucent* – in other words, you can see the legs through them, but not real clearly.

Ichneumon Fly

Order Hymenoptera
Family Ichneumonidae

Ichneumons (sometimes called ichneumonflies) are a large family of parasitic wasps. This ichneumon lays its egg on the back of an active caterpillar. The larva will burrow into the host, eventually killing it. Probably it won't kill the host until the caterpillar has made a cocoon: then the ichneumon larva will have a cozy little home in which to pupate as it feeds on the remains of its host.

STUDY the final drawing *before you start!*

Do you see
- *three body parts?*
- *six legs?*
- *two antennae?*
- *wings (how many)?*
- *eyes?*

Does the insect look
- *shiny? smooth? fuzzy?*
- *hard? soft?*

1. Draw ovals for the *thorax* and *head.* Add the shiny eye, and long, gracefully curving antennae.

2. Carefully draw the curving tail, one segment at a time.

3. Add the wings, one showing the curved shape, and the other just a sliver.

4. Draw the legs. Look closely at how they bend before drawing.

6. Add the victim caterpillar. Draw the other three legs.

7. Add veins in the wings, and complete your drawing with shading. Leave some areas white to make the caterpillar look round.

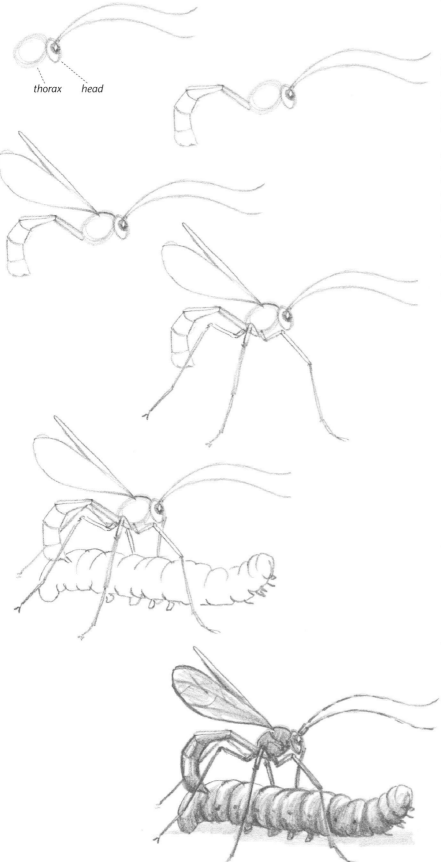

thorax   head

Japanese Beetle

Order Coleoptera
Family Scaribaeidae (scarab beetles)

The Japanese Beetle has been a familiar and widespread pest in the U.S. since its accidental introduction around 1916. Its body and legs are bright metallic green; the elytra (wing coverings) are brown or reddish orange. Larvae feed underground on roots; adults eat foliage, leaves, and fruits of more than 200 kinds of plants. Careful use of parasitic wasps has reduced its numbers in some areas.

STUDY the final drawing *before you start!*

Do you see
- *three body parts?*
- *six legs?*
- *two antennae?*
- *wings (how many)?*
- *eyes?*

Does the insect look
- *shiny? smooth? fuzzy?*
- *hard? soft?*

1. Start by drawing the *elytra* (hard fore wings) and *scutellum.*

2. Add the *pronotum, head,* and eyes.

3. Carefully draw the front legs…

4. …then the middle legs…

5. …and finally the rear legs. Add lines to the *elytra.*

6. Finish by adding shading, or, if you have colored pencils, by coloring the beetle dark green with shiny highlights, except for the *elytra,* which are reddish brown.

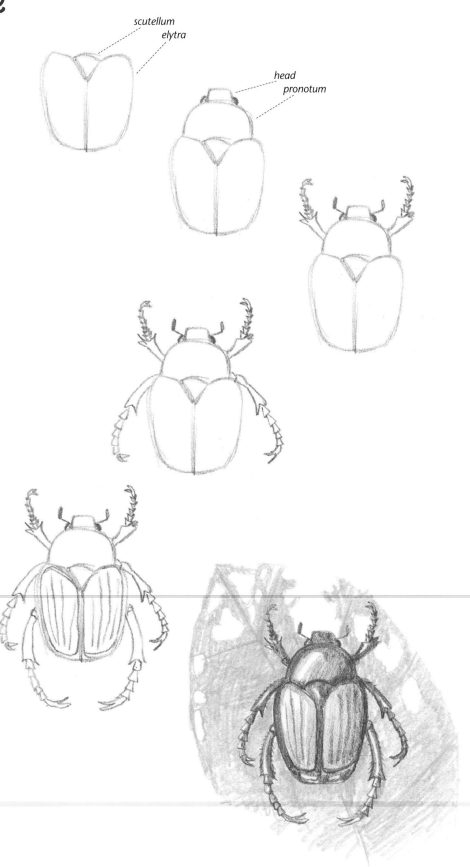

scutellum
elytra

head
pronotum

Lacewing

Order Neuroptera (net-veined insects)
Family Chrysopidae (Green Lacewings)

These common insects don't fly very well, but they're great at eating aphids, so they're welcome in the garden! They lay eggs at the end of tiny stalks, usually on foliage. They pupate in silken cocoons.

STUDY the final drawing *before you start!*

Do you see
- *three body parts?*
- *six legs?*
- *two antennae?*
- *wings (how many)?*
- *eyes?*

Does the insect look
- *shiny? smooth? fuzzy?*
- *hard? soft?*

1. Carefully draw the outline of the wing.

2. Add two main veins…

3. …and then create the pattern of cells inside of them.

4. Now add a row of veins and cells at the top of the wing,

5. and fill in the center section.

6. Draw one more row of cells on the bottom.

7. Add the body and head with its long antennae.

8. Draw the legs. Lightly shade a bit in the wings.

Lovely lacewing!

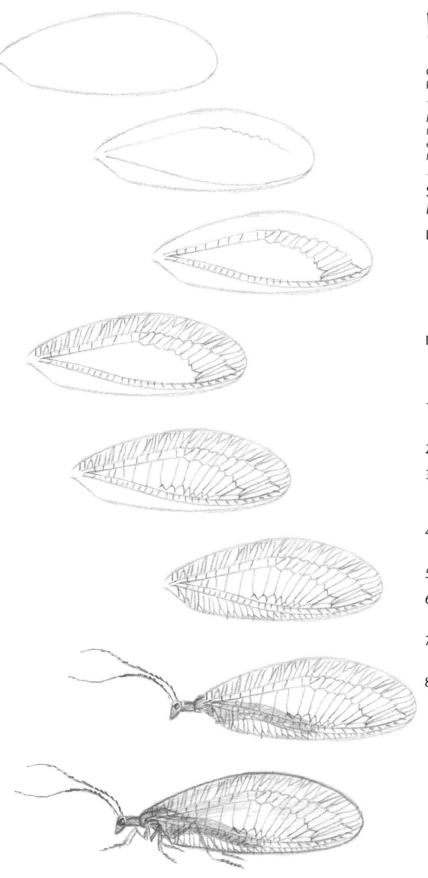

Draw Insects   29

Ladybug Beetle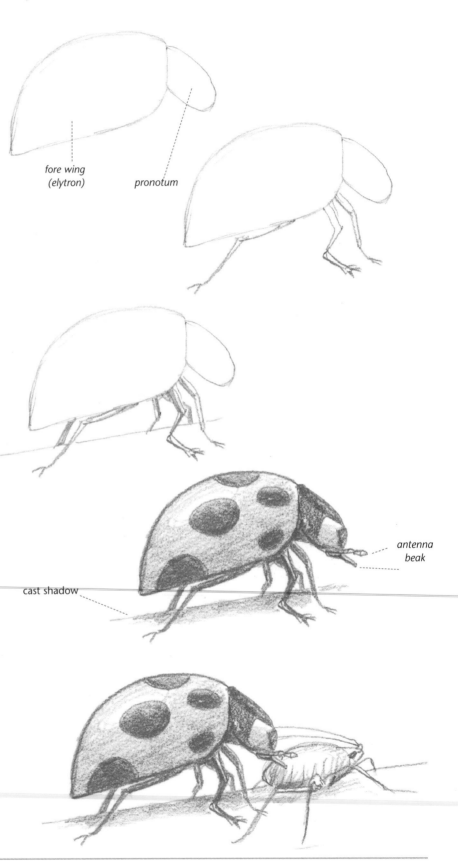

Order Coleoptera
Family Coccinellidae

*Labybugs, also called Ladybirds, are
welcome in the garden because they feed
on aphids. They also eat scale insects
and mites which otherwise damage
plants*

STUDY the final drawing
before you start!

Do you see
 • *distinct body parts?*
 • *six legs?*
 • *antenna?*
 • *wing?*

Does the insect look
 • *shiny? smooth? fuzzy?*
 • *hard? soft?*

1. Draw the *fore wing* and the
   shape that looks like the
   head, but is actually the
   pronotum, which covers the
   head.

2. Add the front, middle, and
   rear leg.

3. Make a line for the edge of
   the stem, and draw the
   other three legs.

4. Add spots on the front wing
   and *pronotum.* Draw the
   *antenna (one of two; the
   other you can't see),* and the
   beak. Add shading and a
   cast shadow.

5. And now *(YES!!)* make the
   ladybug sucking the life out
   of an aphid.

   Guten appetit, ladybug!

fore wing
(elytron)

pronotum

antenna
beak

cast shadow

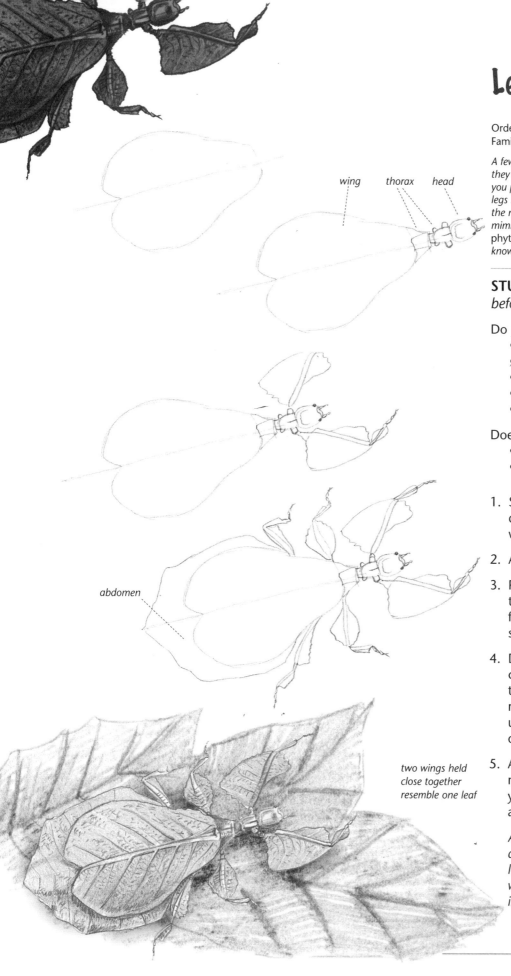

Leaf Insect

Order Phasmatodea
Family Phylliidae (leaf insects)

A few insects imitate plants so well that they won't move during the day, even if you pick them up! They can also drop legs if necessary, then grow them back the next time they molt. The ability to mimic plant structure is called phytomimesis *(thought you'd want to know).*

wing   thorax   head

STUDY the final drawing *before you start!*

Do you see
- *three body parts?*
- *six legs?*
- *two antennae?*
- *wings (how many)?*
- *eyes?*

Does the insect look
- *shiny? smooth? fuzzy?*
- *hard? soft?*

1. Starting with a center line, draw the pear-shaped wings.

2. Add the *thorax* and *head.*

3. From the first segment of the thorax, draw two skinny front legs, then add the leaf shape to them.

4. Draw the middle legs connecting to the second thorax segment, and the rear legs sticking out from under the wings. Add the outline of the *abdomen.*

abdomen

5. Add lines and shading to make it look like a leaf! Take your time, and look closely at the example for ideas.

   Add camouflage! Draw sticks and leaves, so that someone looking at your drawing won't even know there's an insect there....

two wings held close together resemble one leaf

Locust

Order Orthoptera
Suborder Caelifera

Certain grasshoppers are called locusts, from the Latin word for grasshopper. Only nine of 5,000 species of the suborder Caelifera make mass migrations, but when they do, they eat all vegetation in their path. There's the Old Testament plague of locusts descending on Egypt; in modern times trains have been delayed during locust migrations because the tracks were "slimy" from dead insects. Grasshopper Glacier in Montana is full of dead locusts. In the US in the 1870s, a single swarm was estimated to contain 124 billion insects.

STUDY the final drawing *before you start!*

Do you see
   • *three body parts?*
   • *wings (how many)?*
   • *six legs?*

1. Start with two small circles and a longer, rectangular shape for the *head, thorax,* and *abdomen.*

2. Draw the two front legs stretched out either side. Add details to the head, and antennae.

3. Add the second, short pair of legs pointing backwards, and the much longer rear legs. Draw short curved lines for the abdominal segments.

4. Carefully outline the wings.

5. Now add about a zillion little veins and cells. Take your time–it's worth it! Add shading and texture to the body.

head   thorax   abdomen

head

thorax

abdomen

Head Louse

Order Anoplura
Pediculidus humanus humanus

This louse glues little white eggs, called nits, to hair, usually on the back of the head. (Now you can figure out where the term "nit-picking" comes from.) Head lice can be easily transmitted from one person to another. Lice are sometimes called 'cooties.'

STUDY the final drawing *before you start!*

Do you see
  • *three body parts?*
  • *six legs?*
  • *two antennae?*
  • *wings?*
  • *eyes?*

Does the insect look
  • *shiny? smooth? fuzzy?*
  • *hard? soft?*

1. Draw a small circle for the *head,* a larger oval for the *thorax,* and a much larger oval for the *abdomen.´*

2. Carefully divide the abdomen into segments, and add the little bits at the tail end.

3. Mark the thorax to show where three pairs of legs attach, and draw the rear legs…

4. …then the middle legs…

5. …and finally the front legs. Add more details to the head.

6. Finally, add shading, little bristly hairs and a few little human hairs to hold on ´to.

Cute cootie!

Luna Moth

Order Lepidoptera
Family Saturniidae (giant silkworm moths)

This beautiful pale green moth is only found in North America, and is considered endangered. Many have been killed by pesticides and pollutants.

STUDY the final drawing *before you start!*

Do you see
- *three body parts?*
- *six legs?*
- *two antennae?*
- *wings (how many)?*
- *eyes?*

Does the insect look
- *shiny? smooth? fuzzy?*
- *hard? soft?*

1. Draw a cocoon-shaped oval for the body, and add two feathery antennae.

2. Carefully (and lightly) draw one fore wing.

3. Carefully (and lightly) add the other fore wing.

4. Draw the hind wings, with their long tails. Go slowly; turn your paper if it helps you draw the curves.

5. Add wing veins, spots, shading and texture. (If you have colored pencils, shade it a light green color. The large *costal vein* is maroon.)

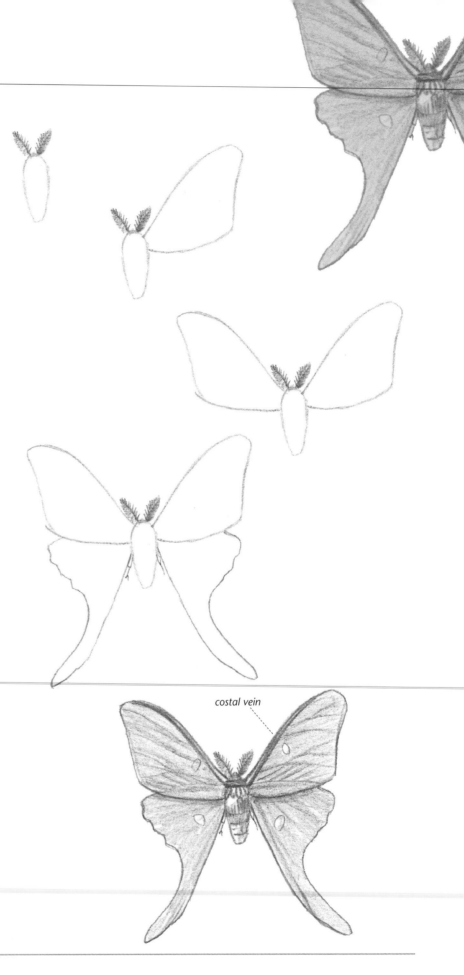

costal vein

Mosquito

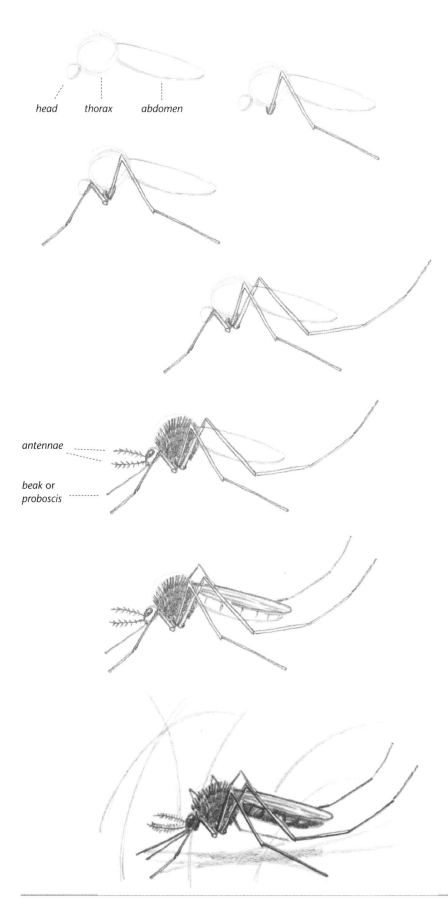

head   thorax   abdomen

antennae

beak or proboscis

Order Diptera
Family Culicidae

You can tell this is a female mosquito because it has only a few hairs on the antennae (on males, they're more feathery), and lacks the male's two additional beak-like palps. Only the females bite. Mosquitoes can convey diseases such as malaria, generally only in tropical areas.

STUDY the final drawing *before you start!*

Do you see
  • *three body parts?*
  • *six legs?*
  • *two antennae?*
  • *wings (how many)?*
  • *eyes?*

1. First, make some high-pitched, whining noises to get in the mood.... Now draw the *head, thorax,* and *abdomen.*

2. Add the middle leg...

3. ...the front leg...

4. ...and the hind legs, curving up into the air.

5. Draw the eye and *antennae,* and the *beak,* or *proboscis,* ready to do business. Add texture to the thorax.

6. Add the wing, covering part of the abdomen, and the lines for abdominal segments. Draw the other hind leg.

7. Add the other two legs, and shading, a bit of cast shadow and a few human hairs.

Moth in flight

Order Lepidoptera
Family Noctuidae (Noctuid moths)

Most moths are active at night, in contrast to butterflies, which fly only during the day. All but a very few moths suck nectar through their curved proboscis; one primitive group has jaws for eating pollen. Unlike butterflies, moths rest with their wings like a roof over their bodies, flat over their bodies, or flat against a support.

STUDY the final drawing *before you start!*

Do you see
- *three body parts?*
- *six legs?*
- *two antennae?*
- *wings (how many)?*
- *eyes?*

Does the insect look
- *shiny? smooth? fuzzy?*
- *hard? soft?*

1. Draw a small circle for the head, a smaller circle for the eye, and a larger oval for the *thorax.*

2. Add long antennae, and the front *leg.*

3. Draw middle and rear leg.

4. Add the *abdomen,* and the *hind wing,* showing the vein pattern in the wing.

5. Draw the *fore wing* and its main veins.

6. Carefully add shading to make the pattern in the wings. Now add shading, details and texture to the body.

Mahvellous moth!

thorax

leg

hind wing

abdomen

fore wing

Mud Dauber

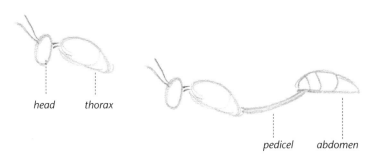

head   thorax

pedicel   abdomen

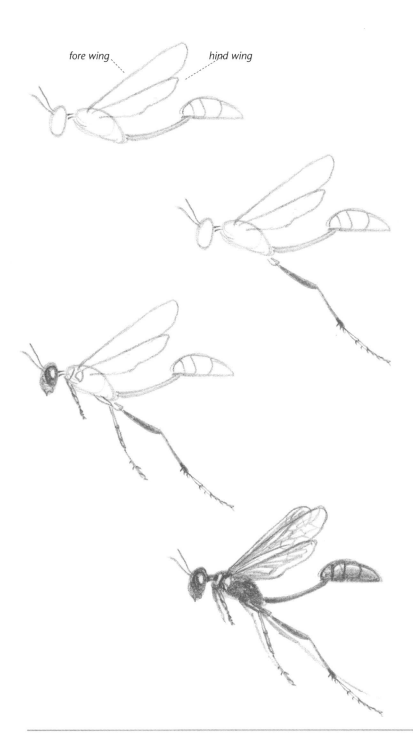

fore wing   hind wing

Order Hymenoptera
Family Sphecidae

Mud daubers are wasps that lay their eggs in tubular cells made from mud. The female paralyzes a spider with venom, stuffs it into a cell for food, lays an egg on top of it, and seals off the cell with mud.

STUDY the final drawing *before you start!*

Do you see
  • *three body parts?*
  • *six legs?*
  • *two antennae?*
  • *wings (how many)?*
  • *eyes?*

Does the insect look
  • *shiny? smooth? fuzzy?*
  • *hard? soft?*

1. Start by drawing the *head,* antennae, short neck, and *thorax.*

2. Add the long, thin *pedicel* and the *abdomen.*

3. Draw the *fore wing* and *hind wing.*

4. Add the long rear leg.

5. Add two more legs. Darken the eye, leaving a white spot to make it look shiny.

6. Lightly draw the three legs on the far side of the body, and add a little bit of the other fore wing. Carefully draw veins in the wings, and add shading.

Looks kind of like a spaceship....

Potter Wasp

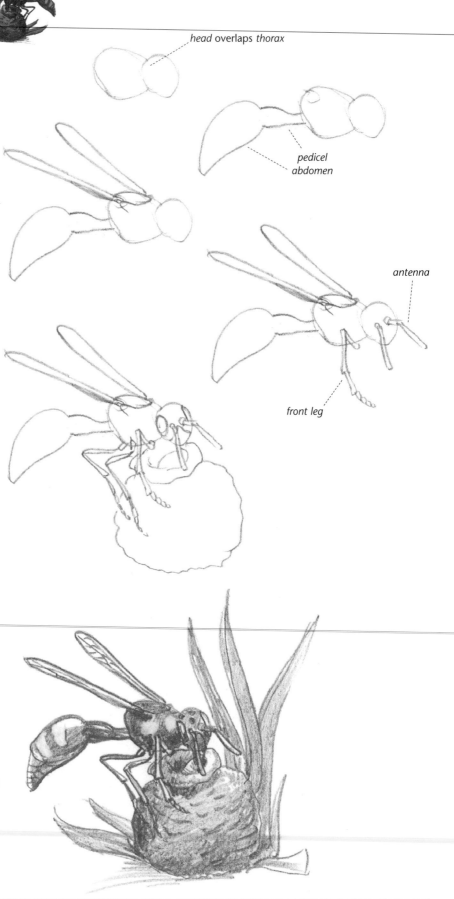

head overlaps *thorax*

Order Hymenoptera
Family Vespidae (Vespid wasps)

Female potter wasps build small chambers that look like little jugs. Inside, they hang an egg from a string. They then sting weevil larvae to paralyze them, and drop them into the chamber for their own larva to eat. These solitary wasps are normally black and yellow.

pedicel
abdomen

STUDY the final drawing *before you start!*

Do you see
- *three body parts?*
- *six legs?*
- *two antennae?*
- *wings (how many)?*
- *eyes?*

antenna

Does the insect look
- *shiny? smooth? fuzzy?*
- *hard? soft?*

front leg

1. Draw the round head *overlapping* the oval-shaped thorax.

2. Add the *pedicel,* then the *abdomen,* a pointed oval.

3. Draw the slender wings.

4. Add jointed *antennae* and *front leg.*

5. Draw eyes and the other two legs, then add the wasp's clay "pot."

6. Add shading, texture, veins in wings and pattern on abdomen. Draw a few blades of grass...

...and perhaps just the slightest glimpse of the weevil larva the wasp is dropping in to feed her own offspring *(yum!).*

Praying Mantis

wing

abdomen

eyes

thorax

Order Mantodea
Family Mantidae

The praying mantis waits in ambush, suddenly moving its spiny fore legs to catch prey. With its strong mouthparts, it can cut through the heads of tough insects like wasps. Its flexible neck means the mantis can turn its head to look at you–a rather eerie feeling! Mantises are cannibalistic; the female often devours the male while mating.

STUDY the final drawing *before you start!*

Do you see
- *three body parts?*
- *six legs?*
- *two antennae?*
- *wings?*
- *eyes?*

Does the insect look
- *shiny? smooth? fuzzy?*
- *hard? soft?*

1. Draw the long *abdomen* and *wing.*

2. Add the *thorax* at a slight angle, then *eyes,* head, and mouthparts.

3. Draw the segments of the front leg, raised and ready to snare prey.

4. Add antennae and the other front leg.

5. Draw the two rear legs. Look carefully at the way each bends.

6. Now add the other two rear legs. Add shading, texture, and details.

And ask yourself, *"What is that insect thinking when it looks at me like that?"*

Pyrgotid Fly

Order Diptera
Family Pyrgotidae

This is not your normal insect attack! The Pyrgotid fly is actually laying its eggs in the back of the flying May beetle. When the eggs hatch, the larvae will feed on the beetle, killing it as they grow larger. Sounds like a science fiction film...

STUDY the final drawing *before you start!*

Do you see
- *three body parts?*
- *six legs?*
- *two antennae?*
- *wings (how many)?*
- *eyes?*

Does the insect look
- *shiny? smooth? fuzzy?*
- *hard? soft?*

1. Draw the *abdomen* and *hind wings* of the flying beetle.

2. Add six legs and the pattern on the abdomen.

3. Draw the *fore wings* or elytra (which, on beetles, don't move in flight). Leave space for the attacker.

4. Add the *head, thorax,* and *abdomen* of the attacker.

5. Draw the wings and antennae of the fly.

6. Add shading with a dull pencil, and go over lines with a sharp pencil, to finish your drawing.

Attack in midair!

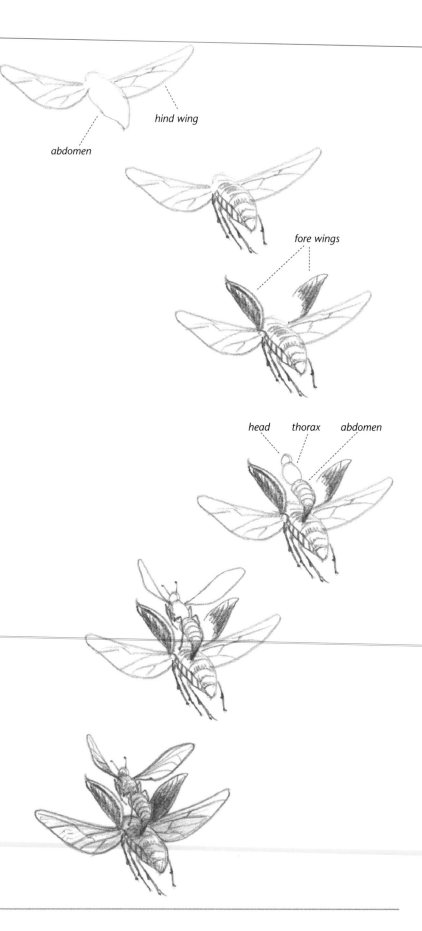

abdomen   hind wing

fore wings

head   thorax   abdomen

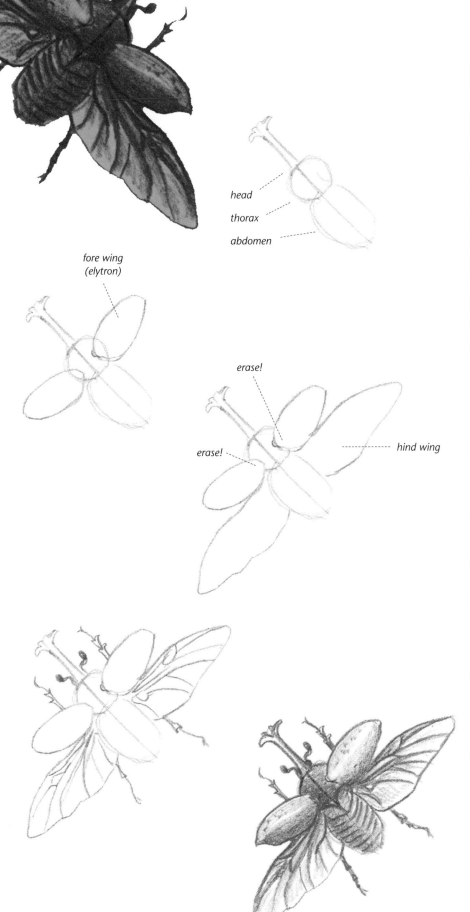

head

thorax

abdomen

fore wing
(elytron)

erase!

erase!

hind wing

Scarab Beetle

Order Coleoptera
Family Scarabaeidae

This is one of about 20,000 kinds of scarab beetle! Some have fabulous metallic colors; others dramatic horns. All have distinctive, clubbed antennae. Ancient Egyptians put scarabs in much of their artwork, and their sun god had a beetle head, since they believed the sun was pushed through the sky the same way a dung beetle rolls a ball of dung along the ground.

STUDY the final drawing *before you start!*

Do you see
- *three body parts?*
- *six legs?*
- *two antennae?*
- *wings (how many)?*
- *eyes?*

Which parts look
- *shiny? smooth? fuzzy?*
- *hard? soft?*

1. Draw the *head* (with long horn), *thorax,* and *abdomen.*

2. Add the protective *fore wings (elytra).*

3. Erase the thorax outline where the front wings overlap it. Draw the *hind wings* (used for flying).

4. Carefully draw the veins in the wings, the front legs and hind legs, and the club-like antennae.

5. Add shading and details...

...cool beetle!

Shieldbug

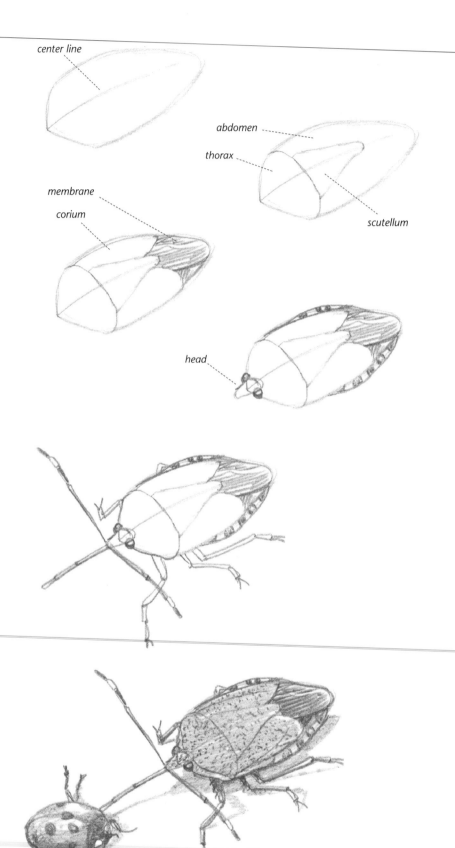

Order Hemiptera (true bugs)
Family Pentatomidae

Ladybugs can deliberately release a little of their own blood when attacked, in a process called reflex bleeding. When predators taste the extremely bitter, bright orange-yellow blood, they learn to associate the bright colors of the ladybug with an undesirable meal. Alas, not this shield bug, which is immune to the toxins in the ladybug's blood, and so reduces our little aphid-killing friend to a desiccated corpse.

STUDY the final drawing *before you start!*

Do you see
- *three body parts?*
- *six legs?*
- *two antennae?*
- *wings (how many)?*
- *eyes?*

Does the insect look
- *shiny? smooth? fuzzy?*
- *hard? soft?*

1. Lightly draw the *center line* and sides of the bug.

2. Divide *thorax* and *abdomen,* and draw the *scutellum.*

3. Add front wings (hiding the hind wings). The thickened base is called the *corium,* the thinner end the *membrane.*

4. Draw *head,* eyes, and checkered sides of the abdomen.

5. Add legs, beak and antennae.

6. Finish your drawing with shading, texture, and *(of course!)* the victim.

center line

abdomen
thorax
membrane
corium
scutellum

head

Silverfish

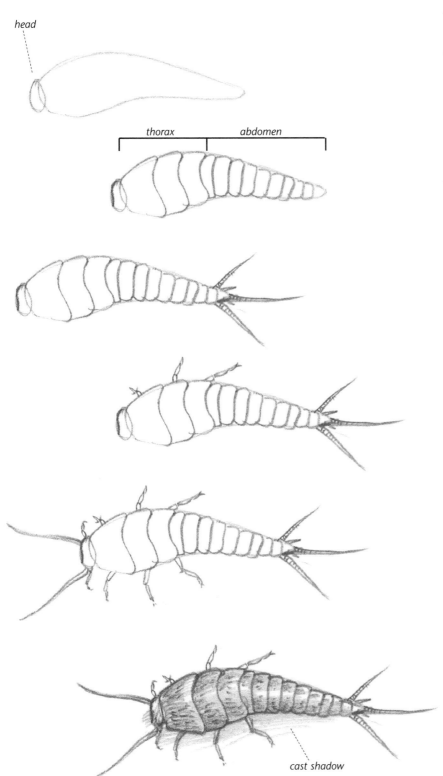

head

thorax *abdomen*

cast shadow

Order Thysanura (common bristletails)
Family Lepismatidae

The scaly covering of the silverfish makes it difficult for ants and spiders to grab it. It lives in warm, dry or damp places such as closets, and can be a pest: it eats starchy stuff, including flour, starch in clothing, and book bindings. It can survive without food for months.

STUDY the final drawing *before you start!*

Do you see
- *three body parts?*
- *six legs?*
- *two antennae?*
- *wings (how many)?*
- *eyes?*

Does the insect look
- *shiny? smooth? fuzzy?*
- *hard? soft?*

1. Start by lightly drawing the long, slightly curved, pointed oval of the body, and a much smaller oval for the *head*.

2. Draw the segments of the *thorax* and *abdomen*.

3. Add the distinctive, three-part bristly tail.

4. Make three little legs on one side.

5. Add three legs on the other side. Draw antennae and the small mouth parts *(maxillary palps)*.

6. Add texture and shading, and a slight *cast shadow*.

Scintillating silverfish!

Springtail

Order Collembola
Suborder Symphypleona

Tiny wingless springtails come in many varieties. Some types of springtail live on ice and snow! The furcula allows this type to jump several inches. Springtails may number several million per acre, scavenging and cleaning up. Usually they're not considered pests.

STUDY the final drawing *before you start!*

Do you see
- *six legs?*
- *two antennae?*
- *wings?*
- *eyes?*

Does the insect look
- *shiny? smooth? fuzzy?*
- *hard? soft?*

1. Draw the *head* with eye, and three *thorax* segments.

2. Add the jointed antenna and front leg.

3. Draw two more legs.

4. Add the *abdomen* and the *furcula.*

5. Draw segments of the abdomen. Add the other antenna and front leg.

6. Add shading and patterns. See if you can make the springtail look shiny by leaving small white spots on the top of the head, thorax, and abdomen.

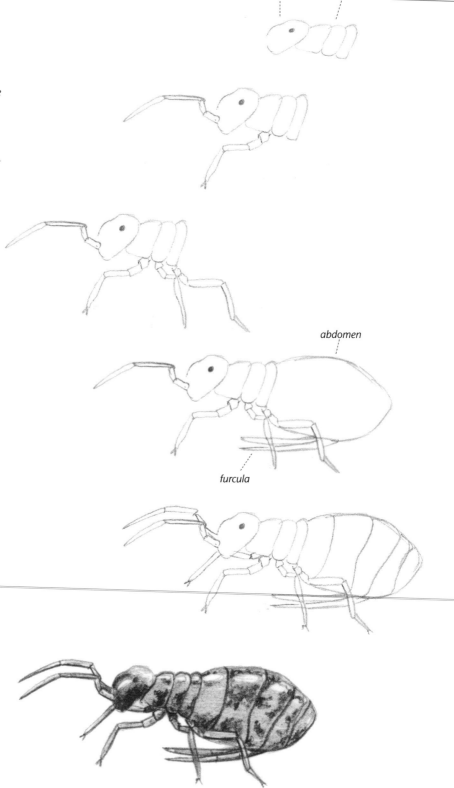

center line

eye

scutellum

thorax   head

end of wing   base of wing

other wing

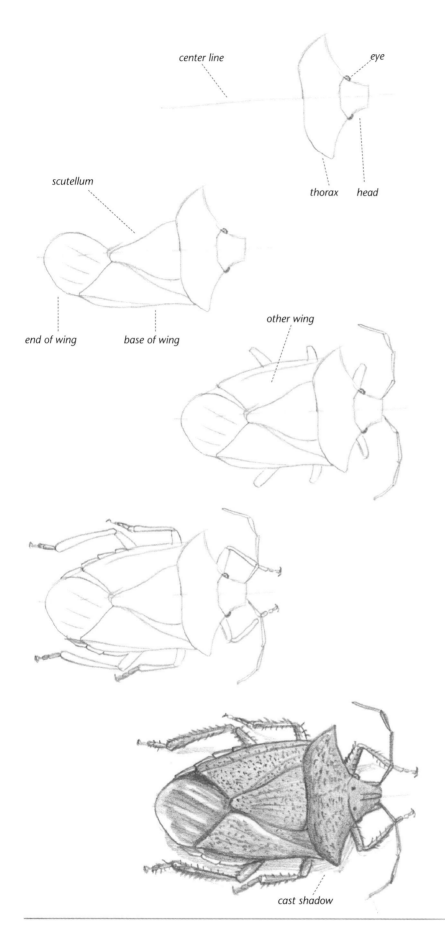

cast shadow

Stink Bug

Order Hemiptera (true bugs)
Family Pentatomidae

Stink bugs release foul-smelling fluid when disturbed. Some stink bugs eat caterpillars and larvae, while others live off plant sap.

STUDY the final drawing *before you start!*

Do you see
- *three body parts?*
- *six legs?*
- *two antennae?*
- *wings (how many)?*
- *eyes?*

Does the insect look
- *shiny? smooth? fuzzy?*
- *hard? soft?*

1. Lightly draw a *center line,* then the stinky *head* with its stinky little *eyes,* and the stinky *thorax.*

2. Add the triangular *scutellum,* and one wing (the *base of the wing* is solid; the *end* is translucent).

3. Draw the *other wing,* antennae, and the first section of each leg.

4. Complete the legs.

5. Finish your drawing by adding shading, details, and texture. With a dull pencil, make a *cast shadow.*

Termite (worker)

Order Isoptera

Most termite species feed on wood, which they can digest because of special microorganisms in their intestines. Termites can be very destructive to buildings. Like ants, they have a highly evolved society, with workers, soldiers, and a reproductive caste which has wings. Some species even have a special caste with nozzles in their heads for secreting a fluid to build and repair nests. With this nozzle, they can spray repellent at invaders. Beware, ants!

STUDY the final drawing *before you start!*

Do you see
   • *three body parts?*
   • *six legs?*
   • *two antennae?*
   • *wings?*
   • *eyes?*

Does the insect look
   • *shiny? smooth? fuzzy?*
   • *hard? soft?*

1. Draw the *abdomen, thorax,* and *head.*

2. Divide the thorax into three sections.

3. Carefully draw a pair of legs attached to each section.

4. Divide the abdomen into ten sections.

5. Draw antennae, *mandibles* and other details of the head. Add light shading and little hairs.

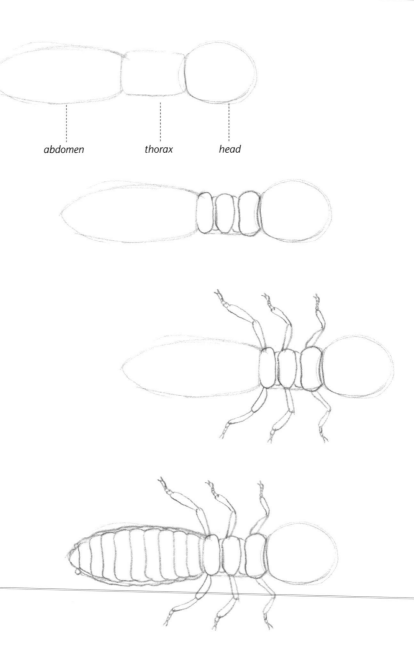

abdomen   thorax   head

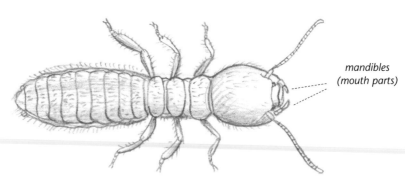

mandibles
(mouth parts)

Tiger Beetle

Order Coleoptera
Family Cicindelidae

Tiger beetles are usually shiny metallic colors. You'll find them in bright sunlight in sandy areas. They run fast and fly fast, and are ferocious predators with their sharp mandibles (jaws). They're hard to catch, which is just as well: some of them have a painful bite.

STUDY the final drawing *before you start!*

Do you see
- *three body parts?*
- *six legs?*
- *two antennae?*
- *wings?*
- *eyes?*

Does the insect look
- *shiny? smooth? fuzzy?*
- *hard? soft?*

1. Start with two half circles for the eyes, tilting away from each other.

2. Add the outline of the head. Look carefully at the shape before you draw.

3. Darken the eyes, leaving a light spot in each. Draw the rounded shape of the *thorax.* Add the long, segmented antennae.

4. Draw the sickle-like mouth parts, and the front two legs on each side.

5. Add the *elytra* (fore wings) and the rear legs.

6. Finish your drawing with shading, patterns, and little bristly hairs.

Looks like something out of a science fiction movie!

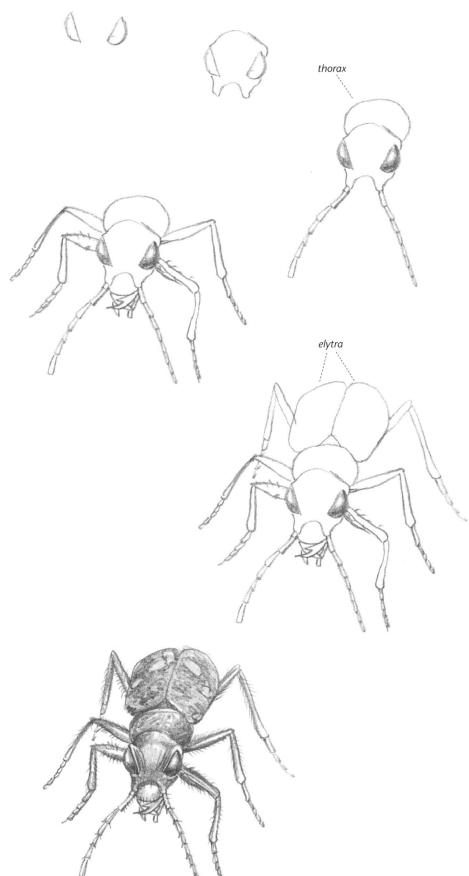

thorax

elytra

Tree Hopper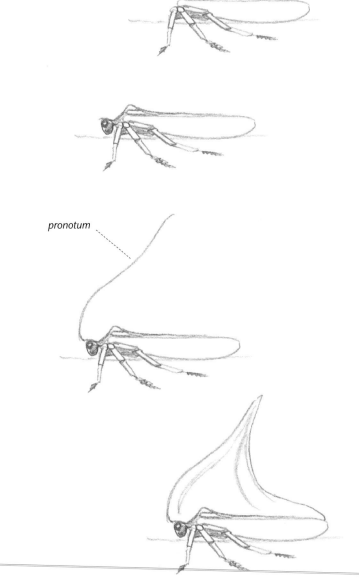

Order Homoptera
Family Membracidae

Treehoppers have an extended pronotum *(upper front section of thorax) that makes them look like a thorn. This protects them from predators. Treehoppers eat sap from plants. This species is bright green with red stripes.*

STUDY the final drawing *before you start!*

Do you see
- *three body parts?*
- *six legs?*
- *two antennae?*
- *wings (how many)?*
- *eyes?*

Does the insect look
- *shiny? smooth? fuzzy?*
- *hard? soft?*

1. Draw a horizontal line for the plant stem. Draw three segmented legs and the long wing.

2. Add the head and shiny eye.

3. Draw a long, curving line for the front of the *pronotum* (top front of thorax).

4. Add the rear curve of the *pronotum,* and lines which are part of its camouflage.

5. Add shading and texture, including veins in the wings. Draw a *real* thorn to give the treehopper something to blend in with, so it won't become a snack for some passing bird.

pronotum

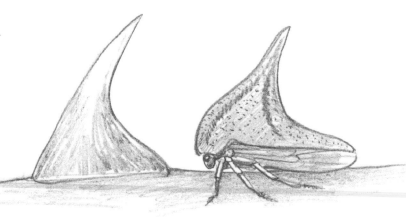

Walkingstick

Order Phasmatodea
Family Phasmidae

Walkingsticks stay still during the day, doing what they do best: looking like a twig so they won't get eaten. They're so good at imitating twigs that they won't defend themselves or try to flee if handled. They can regenerate lost legs. They feed on foliage. Females drop single eggs to the ground, where they hatch in the spring.

STUDY the final drawing *before you start!*

Do you see
- *three body parts?*
- *six legs?*
- *two antennae?*
- *wings (how many)?*
- *eyes?*

Does the insect look
- *shiny? smooth? fuzzy?*
- *hard? soft?*

1. Draw a little tilted pencil.

2. Add a long, slender leg…

3. …and another…

4. …and a couple more…

5. …and a couple more. Draw a twig underneath.

6. Draw antennae and abdominal segments.

7. Add a little shading, and *voila!*

Draw more twigs. See if you can make your walkingstick completely camouflaged!

Wart Biter

Order Orthoptera
Family Tettigoniidae

This European species may bite if you pick it up, at the same time vomiting brown stomach juices (cool trick!). Named in Sweden 200 years ago, it was believed that the bite-and-juice combo removed warts from skin. Apparently this folk remedy was still being used as recently as the late 1940s...with success...!

STUDY the final drawing *before you start!*

Do you see
- *three body parts?*
- *six legs?*
- *two antennae?*
- *wings (how many)?*
- *eyes?*

Does the insect look
- *shiny? smooth? fuzzy?*
- *hard? soft?*

1. Start with a tilted oval for the head, with a circle inside it for the eye. Add the irregular shape of the *prothorax* (the first thoracic segment).

2. Add the front leg...

3. ...then the middle leg...

4. ...and finally the large rear leg, partly overlapped by the middle leg.

5. Starting from the bottom or the top, draw the body parts and wings.

6. To finish, add shading, texture, and pattern.

"Take me to your wart!"

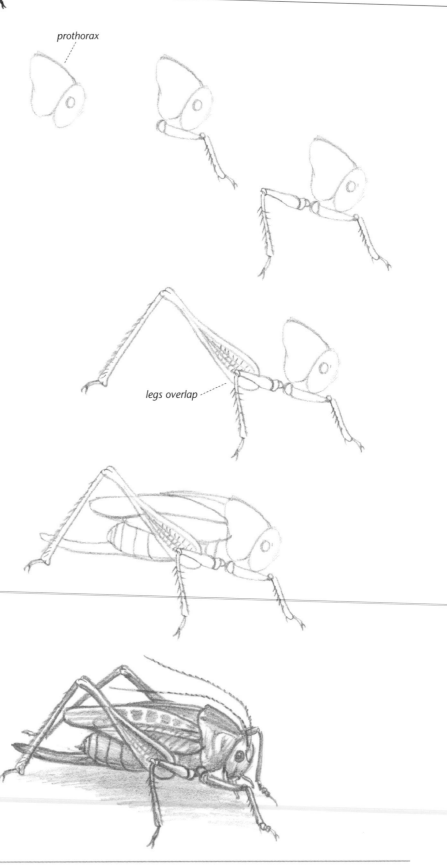

prothorax

legs overlap

Water Strider

Order Hemiptera (true bugs)
Family Gerridae

Water striders run around on the surface of salt and fresh water, feeding on what falls into the water or floats to the surface. Some varieties have wings and some don't.

STUDY the final drawing *before you start!*

Do you see
- *three body parts?*
- *six legs?*
- *two antennae?*
- *wings?*
- *eyes?*

Does the insect look
- *shiny? smooth? fuzzy?*
- *hard? soft?*

1. Draw the *body* and *wings* at a slight angle. Add eyes.

2. Draw antennae.

3. Add the Z-shaped front legs.

4. Draw the much longer middle legs, extending far forward. Remember there are at least three segments in each.

5. Draw the back legs.

6. Add shading and details (don't forget the veins in the wings!), and add little oval ripples and a bit of reflection.

What would it be like if you could walk on water?

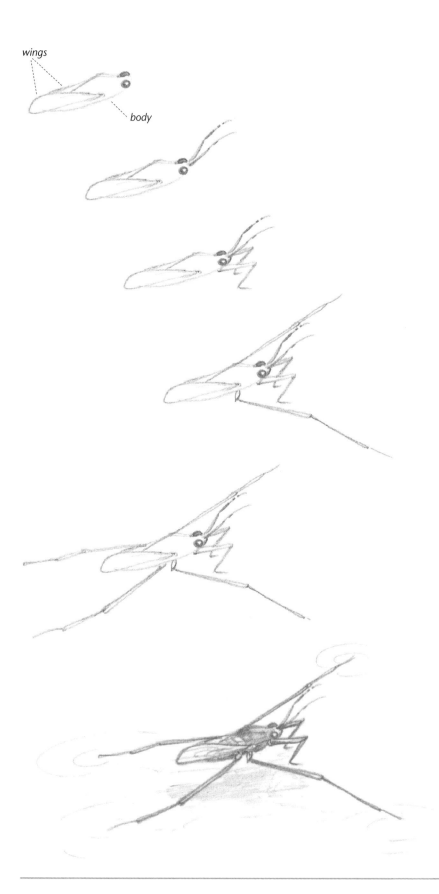

wings

body

Yellow Jacket

Order Hymenoptera
Family Vespidae

Yellow jackets are wasps that live underground, carry off food from picnics, and can sting repeatedly if you "bug" them at all. If you can find their nest, you can put a clear bowl over the opening and leave it there; they become confused, don't figure how to escape and starve to death. This sounds really cruel, unless you've been stung by a yellow jacket,or two, or three…or by one several times in a row….

STUDY the final drawing *before you start!*

Do you see
- *three body parts?*
- *six legs?*
- *two antennae?*
- *wings (how many)?*
- *eyes?*

Does the insect look
- *shiny? smooth? fuzzy?*
- *hard? soft?*

1. Draw a vertical oval for the head, with a pointed end facing down. Add two antennae.

2. Add *thorax* and *abdomen*.

3. Draw the wing and rear leg.

4. Add the middle and front legs. Include all the small segments!

5. Carefully sketch the pattern on the abdomen, and the lines of the *eye* and face.

6. Shade the patterned abdomen, fuzzy thorax and head. Shade the eye, leaving a light highlight to make it look shiny.

   Now tell this thing to get away from me!

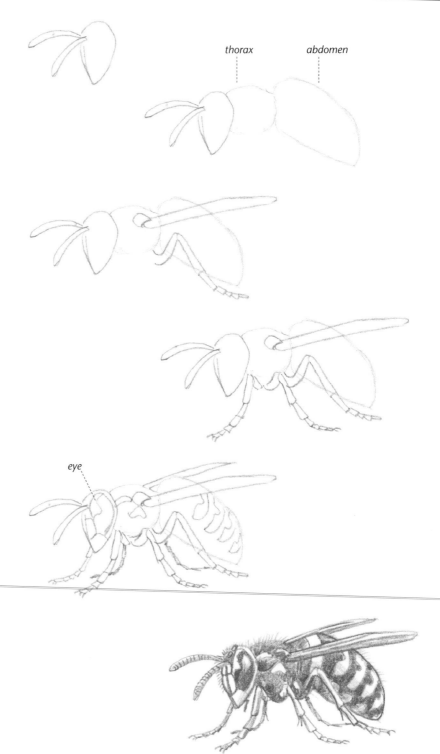

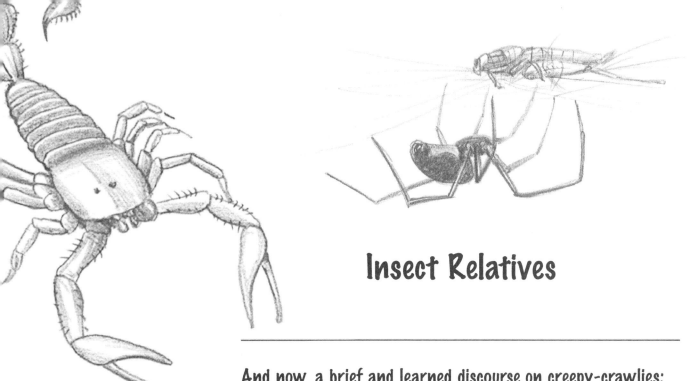

Insect Relatives

And now, a **brief** and **learned** discourse on creepy-crawlies:

As you'll recall from an earlier Brief and Learned Discourse, the primary distinguishing characteristic of members of the class *Insecta* in the phylum *Arthropoda* is the presence of six legs.

In other words, insects have **6 legs!! 6 legs!! 6 legs!!**

So, if a creepy-crawly **does not** have **6 legs**, what is it?

In the phylum *Arthropoda,* along with the class *Insecta,* you'll find a class *Arachnida* (arachnid: think spider), which includes eight-legged spiders, scorpions, mites, ticks, and daddy-long-legs (to name just a few).

Think of a school as a *phylum.* Inside the school there are classrooms, or *classes.* All the children with eight legs go to this *class,* all the children with six legs go to this (very big) *class,* and so on. And the difficult children with too many legs to count (especially because they *never sit still!!!)* go to another *class* called Myriapoda.

Obviously, I can't tell you everything there is to know about scientific classification.

Just remember this: they're all relatives.

Any one of them might show up at your birthday party.

OK, class dismissed!

You may now draw…

Wolf Spider

Order Araneae
Family Lycosidae (wolf spiders)

Wolf spiders usually live on the ground, either in a burrow, under a rock, or sometimes with no home at all. Females make a round egg sack which she drags around with her until the spiderlings hatch. Wolf spiders hunt at night. Their mottled colors make them hard to see among dead leaves and stones.

STUDY the final drawing *before you start!*

Checklist:

Do you see:
- *two body parts?*
- *eight legs?*
- *two pedipalps?*
- *eyes?*

Does it look
- *shiny? smooth? fuzzy?*
- *hard? soft?*

1. Draw a curve for the top of the head. Draw two big eyes, and six smaller eyes.

2. Add the *jaws (chelicerae)* and *pedipalps.*

3. To the sides of the body, draw three segments of the front legs.

4. Complete these legs.

5. Add the second set of legs, partly invisible where the front legs *overlap* them.

6. Draw two more pairs of legs, and the rounded *abdomen.*

7. Finish your drawing by carefully adding shading, texture, and a *cast shadow.*

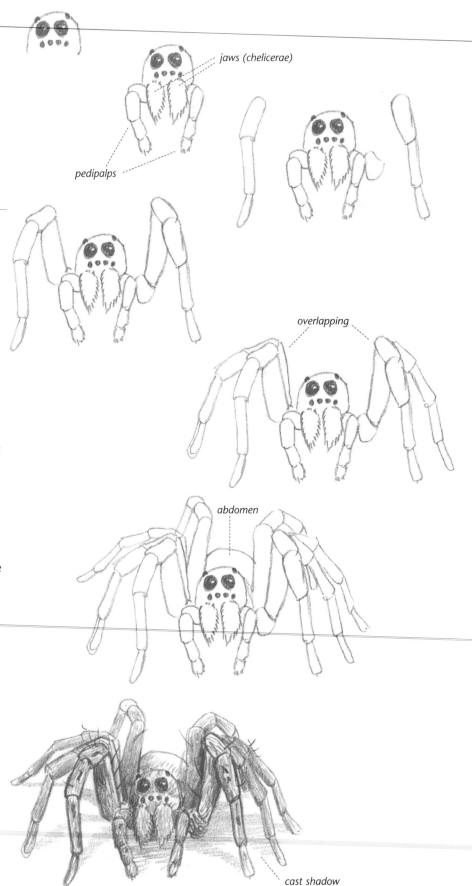

Black Widow Spider

Order Araneae
Family Theridiidae (comb-footed spiders)

This feared spider with the red hourglass shape on its abdomen usually tries to flee rather than attack. Males don't bite. Females often eat males after mating, which is why they're called "widows."

STUDY the final drawing *before you start!*

<u>Checklist:</u>

Do you see:
- *two body parts?*
- *eight legs?*

Does it look
- *shiny? smooth? fuzzy?*
- *hard? soft?*

1. Draw the pointed oval of the *abdomen* with its distinctive *hourglass design,* then add the small, flat oval of the *cephalothorax.*

2. Draw one leg…

3. …and another…

4. …and another…

5. …and another.

6. Now add the visible portions of the other four legs.

7. Finish your drawing by shading the spider black. Add a few lines to suggest a web, and a dead grasshopper (or other insect of your choice) for the black widow's meal.

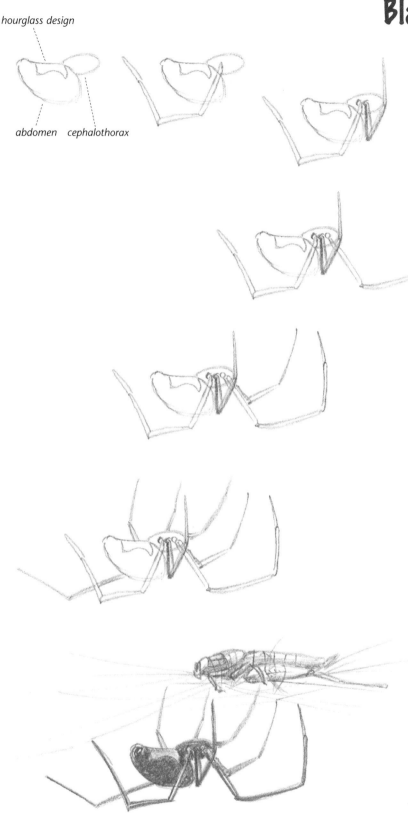

hourglass design

abdomen   cephalothorax

Scorpion

Order Scorpionida

Scorpions subdue or kill large insects, spiders, and sometimes lizards with a poisonous stinger. Most don't attack people, but their sting can produce painful swelling. Long ago, scorpion stings were feared as much as a lion's bite. Scorpions hunt at night, under a sky that has a constellation named for them.

STUDY the final drawing *before you start!*

Checklist:

Do you see:
- *two body parts?*
- *eight legs?*
- *two pedipalps?*
- *eyes?*

Does it look
- *shiny? smooth? fuzzy?*
- *hard? soft?*

1. Start by making the main body shapes.

2. Add lines on the *abdomen,* and carefully draw the sections of the tail, with the stinger at the end.

3. Draw a clawed *pedipalp…*

4. …and another.

5. Now add four walking legs, first on one side…

6. …then on the other.

7. Add shading and bristly hairs to complete your drawing.

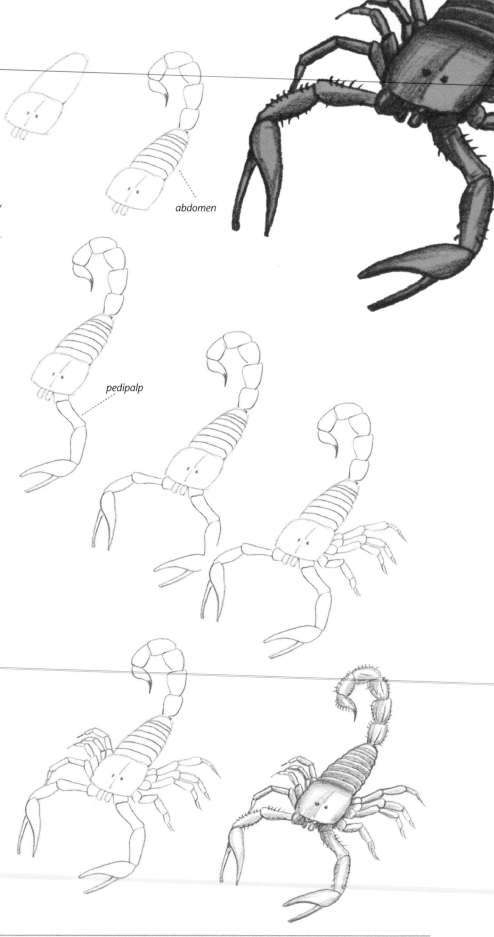

abdomen

pedipalp

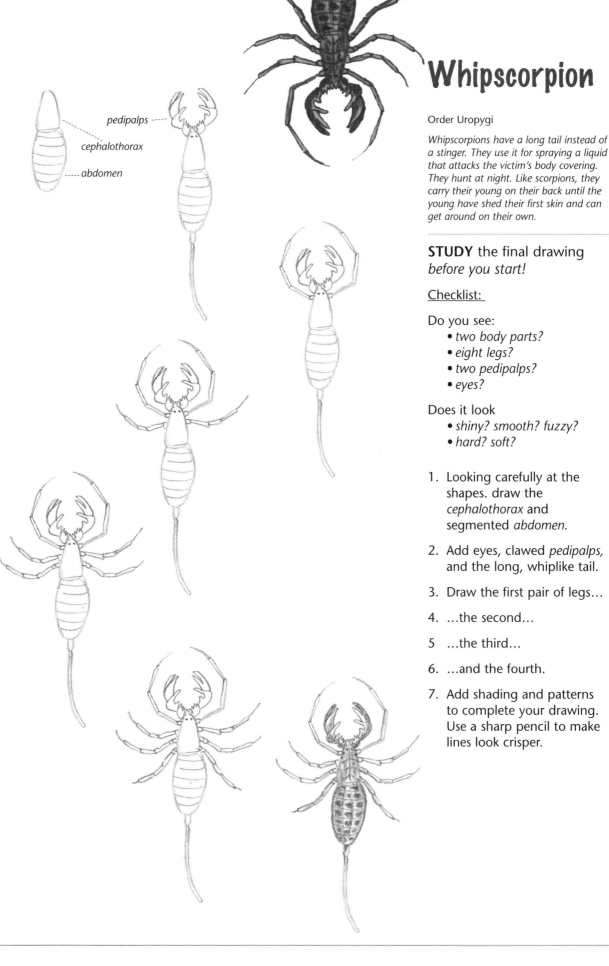

Whipscorpion

Order Uropygi

Whipscorpions have a long tail instead of a stinger. They use it for spraying a liquid that attacks the victim's body covering. They hunt at night. Like scorpions, they carry their young on their back until the young have shed their first skin and can get around on their own.

STUDY the final drawing *before you start!*

Checklist:

Do you see:
- *two body parts?*
- *eight legs?*
- *two pedipalps?*
- *eyes?*

Does it look
- *shiny? smooth? fuzzy?*
- *hard? soft?*

1. Looking carefully at the shapes. draw the *cephalothorax* and segmented *abdomen.*

2. Add eyes, clawed *pedipalps,* and the long, whiplike tail.

3. Draw the first pair of legs…

4. …the second…

5 …the third…

6. …and the fourth.

7. Add shading and patterns to complete your drawing. Use a sharp pencil to make lines look crisper.

pedipalps

cephalothorax

abdomen

Daddy-long-legs

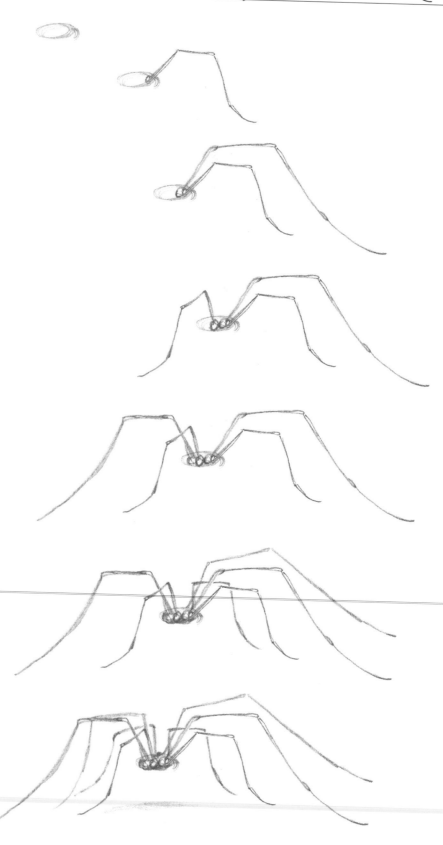

Order Opiliones
Family Phalangiidae (Daddy-long-legs)

Daddy-long-legs feed on small insects and decaying organic matter. Their legs break off easily and don't grow back. Often a number of them gather together, standing with their legs interlaced. A more scientific name for them is phalangids. *The popular name for them in Germany is "tailors."*

STUDY the final drawing *before you start!*

Checklist:

Do you see:
- *two body parts?*
- *eight legs?*
- *two pedipalps?*
- *eyes?*

Does it look
- *shiny? smooth? fuzzy?*
- *hard? soft?*

1. Draw a flat oval to make the body, with tiny mouth parts pointing downward.

2. Add a long, wispy leg…

3. …and another…

4. …and another…

5. …and another…

6. …and…*hey, wait a minute! I've lost count!*

7. Count your legs. No, count the legs in your drawing. When you have eight, you're done. That's all there is to it!

   Unless, of course, you want to draw a gathering of daddy-long-legs, with their legs all interlaced…why not?

cephalothorax   abdomen

Ant-mimic Spider

Order Araneae
Family Clubionidae (sac spiders)

These spiders look surprisingly like ants, and live near ant hills. Their appearance probably confuses predators. They feed on small insects. They are orange, brown, or black, and may have stripes or patterns. They spin tubular resting places inside a rolled leaf, or live under bark or a stone.

STUDY the final drawing *before you start!*

Checklist:

Do you see:
- *two body parts?*
- *eight legs?*
- *two pedipalps?*
- *eyes?*

Does it look
- *shiny? smooth? fuzzy?*
- *hard? soft?*

1. Draw the *cephalothorax* and *abdomen.* Notice how the abdomen is shaped so it looks like both the thorax and abdomen of an ant.

2. Draw the end of the closest leg…

3. …then connect it to the body. Draw the rear leg.

4. Add another leg…

5. …and another…

6. …and then all four legs on the other side of the spider.

7. Finish by shading, leaving parts of the body light to make it look shiny. Add a little shadow and a few spots to suggest dirt or sand.

    Nice ant…uh, spider!

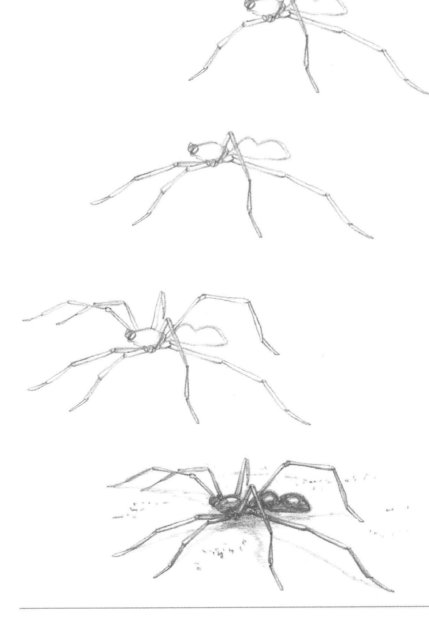

Tick

Order Acarina

Family Ixodidae

Ticks feed on the blood of mammals, swelling to many times their size as they fill up. They then drop off to lay hundreds of eggs, and look for another host. They anchor themselves in the skin with a pointed probe with backwards-facing teeth. This is so strong that if you try to simply pull a tick off, you'll probably break off the head, which stays in the skin.

STUDY the final drawing *before you start!*

Checklist:

Do you see:
- *two body parts?*
- *eight legs?*
- *two pedipalps?*
- *eyes?*

Does it look
- *shiny? smooth? fuzzy?*
- *hard? soft?*

1. Start with a pair-shaped body, and little head and mouth parts.

2. Add a pair of segmented legs to help it hold on while it sinks its head into skin…

3. …and another two pairs…

4. …and yet another pair *(you know it's not an insect now, since it has too many legs).*

5. Finish your drawing by adding shading and texture.

   Or try drawing your tick as it looks after feeding on blood for a while…it will get bigger still before dropping to the ground.

   Yuck!

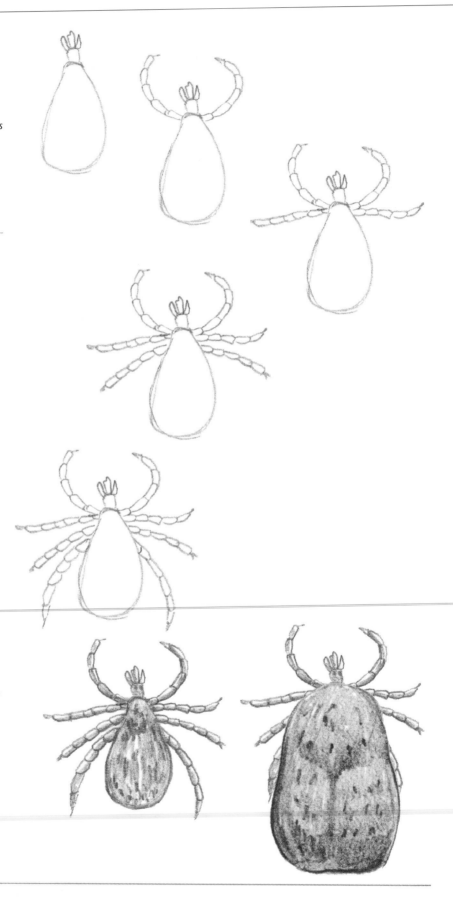

Mite

Order Acarina
Family Trombidiidae

There are perhaps 20,000 species of mites worldwide. Most are tiny, and they have a variety of shapes. Some are beneficial, feeding on aphid eggs; others feed on plants and weaken them. Velvet mites are bright red. Their parasitic larva attacks insects, spiders, daddy-long-legs, and scorpions.

STUDY the final drawing *before you start!*

Checklist:

Do you see:
- *two body parts?*
- *eight legs?*
- *two pedipalps?*
- *eyes?*

Does it look
- *shiny? smooth? fuzzy?*
- *hard? soft?*

1. Begin by drawing a small circle sitting on top of a much larger oval.

2. Add circular bulges either side of the little circle, triangles for the head, feelers and mouth parts.

3. Draw the first pair of segmented legs, up and out from the head.

4. Add the second pair, pointing more to the side.

5. Draw two more pairs.

6. Add shading and texture.

Idea! Create a cartoon character called

Mighty Mite!

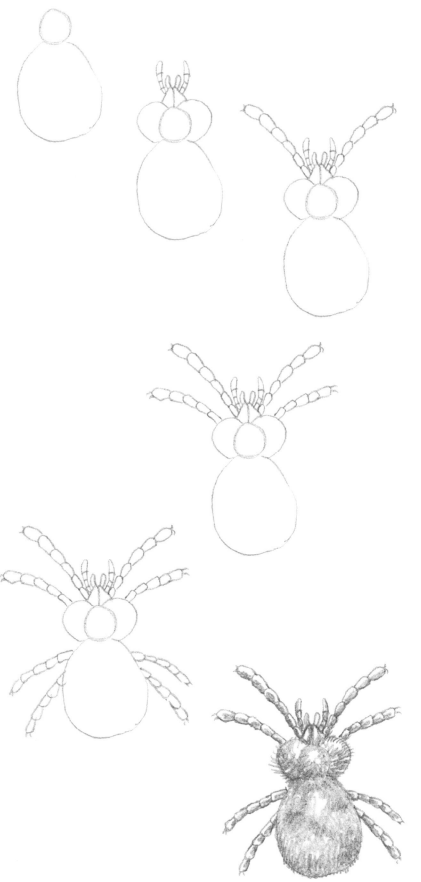

Centipede

Order Scolopendromorpha

Centipedes run quickly with either 21 or 23 pairs of legs. They usually live under stones. The largest centipedes, like this one, live in tropical and subtropical areas. They are dangerous; their bite is very painful.

STUDY the final drawing *before you start!*

Checklist:

Do you see:
- *22body parts?*
- *42 legs?*
- *two pedipalps (feelers)?*
- *eyes?*

Does it look
- *shiny? smooth? fuzzy?*
- *hard? soft?*

1. Draw a long, curved worm.

2. Make a small oval area for the head, and draw its little segmented feelers. Then add 20 short, curving lines to make the body segments.

3. Draw the segmented antennae, and the last two legs sticking out the back end of the centipede. Then draw the first pair of legs, and the second…

4. …and on and on, until you have 21 pairs of legs! Add shading, leaving light areas along the top to make the body look shiny.

Sensational centipede! Do you think it would make a good pet?

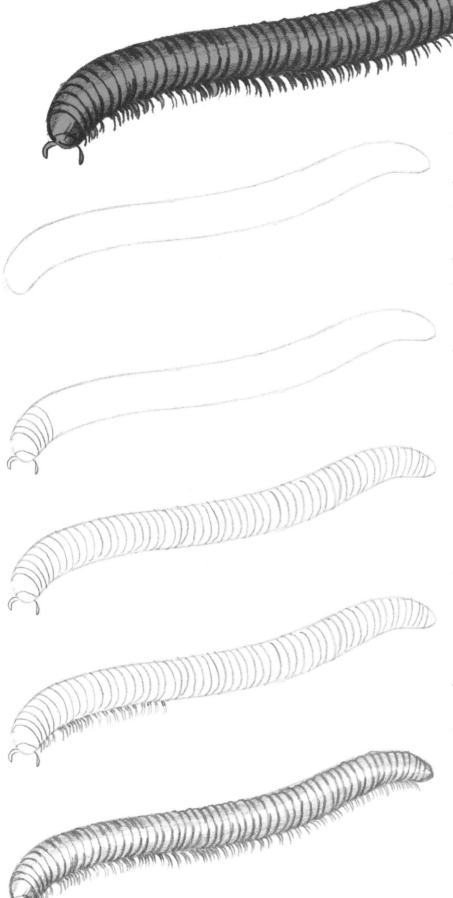

Millipede

Class Myriapoda (air breathing arthropods)

Millipedes have been around for a very long time. This Giant Julid from Africa is part of a family that exists almost unchanged in Africa and South America, strong evidence that the two continents were once joined. Millipedes live in moist areas, and feed mostly on rotting vegetation. Their hard exoskeleton protects them, but most also have chemical defenses.

STUDY the final drawing *before you start!*

Checklist:

Do you see:
- *about a million body parts?*
- *about two million legs?*
- *two pedipalps?*
- *eyes?*

Does it look
- *shiny? smooth? fuzzy?*
- *hard? soft?*

1. Draw a fat, slightly curved worm.

2. Add little feelers, then draw small curved lines for the body segments. Draw them carefully, to make the body look round…

3. …and then add a ton more!

4. Now add little creepy-crawly legs, first a few…

5. …and then a ton more!

Finish your slithering little friend with shading, leaving the middle part of the body light to make it look round.

Magnificent millipede!

Index

Learn about other books in
this series online at
www.drawbooks.com!